The Beatles Files

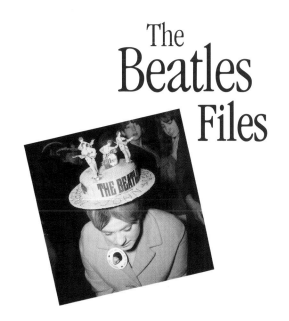

The Beatles Files

Andy Davis

To the Daily Mirror readers having a great time in Tobogo, - wish you were here. John Lennon Ringo Starr

This edition published in 2001
by Greenwich Editions
10 Blenheim Court
London N7 9NY

Reprinted 2002
© Copyright 2001 Salamander Books Ltd.

A member of the Chrysalis Group plc

CREDITS
Commissioning editor: Will Steeds
Project manager: Christopher Westhorp
Design: Phil Smee, Waldo's Design, St. Alban's, UK
Picture research: Hugh Gallacher (Bookman Projects Ltd.), Andy Davis, Phil Smee
Production: Neil Randles, Karen Staff, Ruth Arthur
Colour reproduction: Advance Graphic Services, London

For Bookman Projects Ltd.: Nick Kent, Hugh Gallacher

Printed in Spain
ISBN 0-86288-496-9

Prelim and chapter opener pictures
Title page: The Beatles reading the *Sunday Mirror* backstage at the ABC Cinema in Plymouth, 13 November 1963.
Page 4: A message wired to the *Daily Mirror* from John and Ringo on holiday in Tobago.
Page 5: The boys perform a classic 'Beatle pose' backstage at The London Palladium on 13 October 1963.
Page 6: Filming a sequence for *A Hard Day's Night* at the Scala Theatre.
Page 7: John and Paul in the back of their limousine after a concert.
1963: At the Adelphi Cinema, Slough, on 5 November.
1964: In Blackpool for a concert at the Opera House on 16 August.
1965: Rehearsing *Blackpool Night Out* on 30 July.
1966: On the set of *Top Of The Pops* on 16 June.
1967: Press reception for *Our World* on 24 June.
1968: Press reception for *Yellow Submarine* on 8 July.
1969: Playing live on the Apple rooftop on 30 January.

NOTE
Whenever a significant sum of money is mentioned in the text, its approximate modern-day value has been provided in brackets. The US Dollar values are contemporary ones. If a dollar value is followed by two sterling figures in brackets, these are, unless specifically stated otherwise, the contemporary sterling value and the value of that sterling today – not the value of those 1960s' dollars today.

CONTENTS

Foreword   6

Introduction   7

The Photographers   8

Chapter One   1963   10

Chapter Two   1964   30

Chapter Three   1965   82

Chapter Four   1966   102

Chapter Five   1967   114

Chapter Six   1968   128

Chapter Seven   1969   144

Chronology   157

Acknowledgements and Bibliography   159

FOREWORD

SEEING THESE PICTURES from the *Daily Mirror* archives brings back the whole era: The Beatles were the last black-and-white group, the stark early sixties silhouette, the dapper suits, narrow trousers and straight skinny ties, before Woodstock and the hippies smudged all the sharp edges with psychedelic colours. The early sixties was monochromatic: the newspapers were black-and-white, the television was black-and-white (colour TV was not introduced until 1967). The newspapers still made news. The sound of the sixties was the motor-driven camera, that glamorous whizzing noise, multiplied scores of times, wherever The Beatles went, which now has sinister overtones. Back then it was the youthful sound of swinging London and no one was harmed by it.

The Beatles were on the cusp between old fashioned variety shows and the modern stadium rock concert – which they effectively invented. They appeared with jugglers and acrobats in Paris, and hoofers and comedians on the telly and at the height of Beatlemania found themselves doing Christmas panto, acting out inane sketches each night.

The *Daily Mirror* (and *Sunday Mirror*) realised early on that by running Beatles photographs, the fans would get their parents to buy the *Mirror*, and that the fans only had to grow a little older before they would buy a copy of it each day themselves. The *Mirror* proclaimed itself "switched on" – they were too coy to say "turned on" with its drug connotations. Mirror Group photographers were sent to chronicle every Beatles event: the parties, the concerts, the holidays and films and, because the *Mirror* was so powerful, they had the kind of backstage access that photographers today can only dream of. The results are the treasure trove we see in this book, most of which have never been seen before. From his years with *Beatles Monthly* Andy Davis knows a rare Beatles picture when he sees one and he has done sterling work here.

The Beatles represented the energy of sixties' Britain: youth breaking out of the tight cocoon of post-war austerity, emerging like a glorious butterfly and stretching its wings. It was a new thing, and seeing these pictures is a poignant reminder of how young and inexperienced we all were. British TV was handicapped by union insistence that a full camera crew had to be used for news coverage, so except for the occasional airport arrival, the newspapers still reigned supreme. These are news pictures, not art; they capture the excitement of late-breaking news and still hold that excitement today, more than thirty years later.

BARRY MILES

INTRODUCTION

UNLIKELY AS IT MAY SEEM, an archive containing thousands of unpublished photographs of the most famous group in the world was rediscovered recently, after lying virtually dormant for three decades. It had been housed in a bustling office in central London until the early 1990s, and then moved to an ugly industrial building on the outskirts of Watford. Although belonging to one of Britain's most popular daily newspapers, the *Daily Mirror*, only a small number of photographs from this archive had ever been reproduced, and its true value was scarcely recognised.

The cream of those forgotten images, more than 400 photographs in all, now appear in *The Beatles Files*. It was never a secret that these files existed; indeed, they are the first port of call whenever a Mirror Group paper requires a Beatles photo. But few picture researchers had ever looked beyond the archive's over-worked boxes of dog-eared 10 x 8-inch prints. Fewer still had delved into the numerous files of negatives, which were stuffed into unwieldy envelopes alongside fading contact strips still reeking, thirty years on, of developing chemicals. Closer investigation revealed the *Mirror*'s Beatles archive to be unique, representing the most comprehensive single-source pictorial record of the group in existence. Other collections may be bigger, or more varied, but no other independent organisation photographed The Beatles so often and so consistently as the *Daily Mirror* did in the 1960s and, having done so, managed to preserve the results!

The *Mirror*'s collection spans all but the earliest days of The Beatles' career. The paper's first session with the group took place in late 1963, following the outbreak of Beatlemania, and from then on it enthusiastically documented their every move. Following the American tours of 1964, coverage of most of their overseas visits was confined to airport arrivals and departures, but domestic stories were pursued with a rigorous newshound persistence.

In addition to landmark events like their MBE awards and the release of *Sgt. Pepper*, the *Mirror* covered less familiar, but equally visual, stories. These included their early UK tours, the TV shows *Around The Beatles* and *The Music Of Lennon & McCartney*, as well as "fillers" like John's 1967 visit to the Motor Show, where he was photographed grinning from ear to ear at the wheel of the fastest saloon

car in the world. *The Beatles Files* concentrates on the group's core years from 1963 to 1969. Each picture was taken specifically for the *Mirror* by the paper's own staff photographers or by stringers working for the *Mirror*. These are predominantly news photographs, "hit-and-run" images of the group caught backstage or in concert, on the steps of a plane or posing politely at an official photo-call. Others are opportunistic shots created by quick-witted photographers with four superstars in their sights and just a minute or two to turn the occasion into something memorable – witness the use of props like the fire buckets on the steps of the Liverpool Empire and real-life swords in the grounds of an Irish castle.

These pictures tell the story of The Beatles' rise and fall as vividly as any biography. In 1963 and 1964 they were at the world's beck and call. After 1965 they stopped posing for showbiz-style shots. And after 1967, the *Mirror* found it increasingly difficult to even photograph the four of them together. Only once in the next three years did the paper manage the feat with a telephoto shot of them playing live on the roof of the Apple building in January 1969. Similarly, the various newspapers' reactions to The Beatles, on which this book's text is based, reveal a steady shift from presenting an image of infallible, inseparable moptops to portraying four independently minded individuals with their own views and (apparent) faults.

The *Daily Mirror*'s undying enthusiasm for The Beatles was in keeping with its role as Britain's first and greatest tabloid newspaper. Ever since its launch in 1903, the *Mirror* has championed working-class values, covering popular issues which concerned the Labour-supporting man in the street; "Forward with the People", said the message on its masthead. It sought to entertain its readers while simultaneously educating them.

In November 1963 the paper ran a piece with the headline "Beatlemania: Why It Makes You Tick", in which a psychiatrist bluntly explained the origins of the phenomenon, foretelling the revolution of the Swinging Sixties in the process: "Beatlemania would not have taken on the magnitude it has if there had not been the need to release sexual urges. These urges exist within us and they demand to be taken notice of." Like The Beatles themselves; the *Daily Mirror* had no genuine competitor in the 1960s. In terms of circulation, the *Daily Express* came the closest, followed by the *Daily Mail*. But despite devoting healthy coverage to the group and to popular issues in general, these more staid broadsheets couldn't compete as the *Mirror* sailed ahead with a succession of front covers and scoops such as its own souvenir magazines *The Beatles By Royal Command* and *The Beatles In America*.

The *Mirror*'s nearest tabloid rival was the now-defunct *Daily Sketch*. Like the *Express* and *Mail*, this was a Conservative paper but one aimed further down-market. The *Sketch* put up a good fight, but its circulation seemed puny when compared with the record-breaking 5,000,000 the *Mirror* proudly announced in June 1964, coincidentally at the height of Beatlemania.

For the duration of the 1960s, the *Mirror* thrived as The Beatles did. It was a well-respected, pugnacious paper with an opinion on everything; its "Shock Issues" tackled subjects as diverse as Rachmanism, the menace of pollution in Britain's rivers, cruelty to animals and neglected children. *Mirror* journalists became household names: Peter Wilson, alias "the man they can't gag" and the doyen of Fleet Street's sports writers; agony aunt Marjorie Proops; war correspondent John Pilger; the "hard common sense" of Cassandra (William Connor), with his daily political column; pop writer Don Short; and showbusiness veteran Donald Zec.

The *Mirror* and its weekend counterpart the *Sunday Mirror* loved The Beatles, but it wasn't beyond criticising them. Zec became an early champion of the group but struggled to keep up as the decade wore on and the band became increasingly unconventional. His tirades against John and Yoko in 1969 are particularly memorable.

More important are the pictures themselves. Back in the 1960s, the few images from this collection which made it into the papers appeared on standard *Mirror* newsprint, often after being retouched to compensate for the low-quality reproduction. Here, for the first time, those images and hundreds more, are reproduced in optimum quality from the original negatives, presenting the ultimate pictorial diary of the greatest band in the history of rock'n'roll.

ANDY DAVIS

The Photographers

DURING THE 1960s, the *Daily Mirror* employed around twenty staff photographers, twice as many as today. Most of these photographed The Beatles during the period covered in this book, each attending about three sessions on average. Among those whose work is represented here are Freddie Cooper, William Ellmann, Monty Fresco, Kent Gavin, George Greenwell, Eric Harlow, Bob Hope, Tom King, Charles Ley, Tommy Lea, Cyril Maitland, Arthur Murray, Charles Owens, Peter Stubbs and Bela Zola.

A number of others were more regular Beatle-watchers. These included Freddie Cole, who in 1964 covered the Madame Tussaud's photo-call, early shows on The Beatles' Autumn Tour (at Bradford with Mary Wells, and at Kilburn in London) and Ringo's press conference to announce the removal of his tonsils; and in 1967, the group's trip with the Maharishi to Bangor, North Wales, and the filming of *Magical Mystery Tour*.

Eric Piper took the exclusive pictures of John Lennon and George Harrison at Dromoland Castle in March 1964. He also captured The Beatles backstage with a couple of American fans at the

Fame, and John with his old art school colleague Johnathan Hague; he shot Ringo Starr and Cilla Black in rehearsal at the BBC; and the following year John and Yoko's "Bagism" protest for James Hanratty. He also covered the last live appearance by two Beatles together in the sixties, when John and George played the "Peace for Christmas" concert at London's Lyceum Ballroom.

More by accident than design, the *Mirror*'s most prolific Beatles photographers were Victor Crawshaw and Alisdair MacDonald. Both joined the paper on the same day in 1960 and both still work there today. Victor saw The Beatles as international jet-setters more often than most, after being stationed at London Airport from 1964, while Alisdair was one of the few members of the *Mirror* team to travel abroad with the group. On one of his earliest sessions, he flew to Paris with them for their residency at the Olympia Theatre in January 1964; and in 1960, he accompanied *Mirror* critic Donald Zec to the Netherlands for John and Yoko's bed-in at the Amsterdam Hilton.

That said, none of the paper's staffers specialised in any particular field – there were no

"It was hard to get great pictures of The Beatles playing live because the lighting in those days wasn't very good."

Hammersmith Odeon in January 1965; down-beat stand-in drummer Jimmy Nicol the same year; and took the fashion shots of Pattie Harrison in 1966. His last Beatles shoot was the premiere of *Yellow Submarine* a few years later.

Ray Weaver concentrated on the latter half of The Beatles' career. In 1967 he pictured John and George in fancy dress at a party thrown by Georgie

dedicated Beatles photographers at the *Mirror* – and each man was valued for his versatility. "The best part of photography is being a hit-and-run man", says Alisdair MacDonald. "A general photographer is capable of doing anything. If you specialise, doing nothing but crime or sport or fashion, day in, day out, you start to lose touch with everything else. Most of us could do anything

Alisdair MacDonald

from a fire, to a murder to a cat show. That's the way we worked."

Photographing The Beatles during the hectic mania years might sound like a glamorous job to some, but to Victor Crawshaw it was business as usual. "None of us were pop fans", he admits. "It was just another job, and it was quite hard work. We had excellent cameras. Roliflexes. Wonderful cameras! But you had to get your focus right – there was no such thing as autofocus then. We didn't even have exposure meters. You had to get your exposures right according to the film you were using, and you'd have to know that in your head. You wouldn't have time to go and take a light-meter reading, you just knew what the light was and set it."

"It was hard to get great pictures of The Beatles playing live", adds Alisdair, "because the lighting in those days wasn't very good. They would be

spread across the stage and, being at the back, Ringo was always hidden behind his drums. So to get a good shot of all four of them to illustrate a story, we'd have to go backstage, before or after the performance."

As far as the *Mirror*'s picture editors were concerned, shots of the group in concert usually lost out in the popularity stakes to something far more appealing – the fans! "Nobody was very interested in The Beatles at first", remembers Victor. "The stories weren't so much about them, but what happened around them. We'd mainly stand with our backs to the stage photographing the kids. All the paper wanted to see were these hysterical, swooning girls. We'd do two or three pictures of The Beatles and then concentrate on the fans."

"There was always a problem photographing The Beatles, or any group for that matter", adds Alisdair, "because there were four of them. If you didn't hit them several times, one was likely to have his eyes shut, another might be looking the other way or making a funny face. So you took as many frames as you could to get it right. Hotels, taxis, aeroplanes, they were the expenses. Film was the cheapest product. So you didn't skimp. You just banged away."

The proliferation of early backstage shots, in which The Beatles lined-up in a neat foursome, posed with a copy of a newspaper or mucked about with props, suggests that the photographers had a good relationship with their star subjects. "The Beatles were very good, very funny", confirms Alisdair MacDonald. "Although I thought John Lennon got pissed off very quickly. He had a short fuse. Paul McCartney could get a bit delicate as well. It began to get a bit heavy when they all started getting their lady friends. For instance, I know Jane Asher's father, who was a psychiatrist, didn't like the idea of common journalists banging on his door trying to find out things about her and Paul." Surprisingly, none of the *Mirror* pictures were planned beforehand. "You couldn't set up anything with The Beatles", says Victor. "Absolutely nothing. Everything was taken as you could get it. We used to have to get to the concerts well in advance. I wouldn't say it was a struggle, because they were there to have their pictures taken, but they wouldn't necessarily stop and hang around for long. You weren't given much time at all. You had to be pretty sharp, otherwise they'd be gone. It wasn't usually The Beatles who were the problem, it was the people who surrounded them. They were kept on the go by the police, the managers, the agents. They didn't have the heavies in those days that groups have today, but they still kept them moving."

Alisdair MacDonald confirms the story: "I remember going to Paris with them in 1964. They stayed at the George V hotel while we were in lesser accommodation, along with the rest of Fleet Street and they didn't come out for ages. We didn't like their press officer, Brian Sommerville, as

Victor Crawshaw

touchy with us. It was all knocking stories towards the end. They were getting stressed amongst themselves. The stress came over to us, so everyone started knocking them – they were no longer being helpful to us."

"The Beatles probably thought they were being hounded", muses Victor, "but it was nothing when compared to today. They would really have only been photographed when they were actually doing something, or going somewhere. They wouldn't have had photographers camping out, chasing them. When they came through the airport, they knew what they had to do. They were there. We were there. We took the picture and then they went off. That was the way it was done. We never had any problems with them the way we do with present day pop groups. The difference is that in the sixties, everybody wanted to have their picture taken. Nowadays it is fashionable not to."

Working with The Beatles was a unique experience, remembers Victor. "Nothing like it was seen again until Princess Diana", he says. "No other pop group had that type of reception. I've seen receptions for The Rolling Stones, for Madonna when she came here. The only thing which sticks in my mind as being remotely like it was when old Liberace came through the airport. But his fan club were all over fifty."

As far as the *Mirror* was concerned, concludes Alisdair MacDonald, The Beatles were always priority news. "With The Beatles the pictures always went in the paper", he says. "You could go out and do a baby picture or an animal picture and think, that's the one, that's in, but when you got back to the office they'd say they already had their animal story for the day, or that mine was the wrong shape or whatever, but with The Beatles the pictures went straight in. The *Mirror* loved The Beatles. With them we couldn't fail. They sold papers, and the *Mirror* was *the* paper." ■

"Nothing like it was seen again until Princess Diana. No other pop group had that type of reception."

he was never very helpful to us. But we pushed it and pushed it and finally got them out into the Champs-Elysées. I got them to pose looking at some postcards, and while I was taking the pictures George Harrison said, 'We're glad you came along, we'd been dying to get out!' They didn't know we'd been banging on the door. Sommerville didn't want them to peak too early, probably."

The French media didn't like banging on The Beatles' door either, adds Alisdair. "It's an unwritten rule in France that you always keep the dressing room door open. Being The Beatles, of course, they shut it, and it developed into a fight backstage. You know in the movies how, when someone gets hit over the head with a chair, it breaks into little bits? Well it happened that night in Paris – the bloke went down, but the chair stayed in one piece!"

Victor Crawshaw experienced no such outbursts photographing The Beatles as they travelled in and out of the country via London Airport, but the job was hardly routine. "Quite honestly, it was a pain in the arse whenever they came through", he says. "It just wasn't

straightforward. You'd have all these girls camping out, invading the airport a couple of days before the flight. The police used to try and herd them into specific areas but they'd always hear rumours that something was happening at a different part of the airport and charge off looking for them."

And, as Alisdair MacDonald remembers, once a photographer had got close to The Beatles, the fans wanted to get close to them: "I'd get girls coming up to me saying, 'Have you met The Beatles?' 'Yes', I'd say. 'Who's your favourite?' they'd ask. 'I like them all.' 'Have you actually touched them?' 'Well, I've bumped into them', and as soon as I'd said that they'd start stroking me!"

Once Beatlemania began to die down, so too did the *Mirror*'s access to the group. "We never saw them much after they went off to America", recalls Alisdair. "Mostly only at the airport after that. The same thing happened with them as what happened to the Spice Girls recently. You build them up, and when you start running out of copy, you start knocking them. After all that stuff about The Beatles being more popular than Jesus happened in the States, they started getting

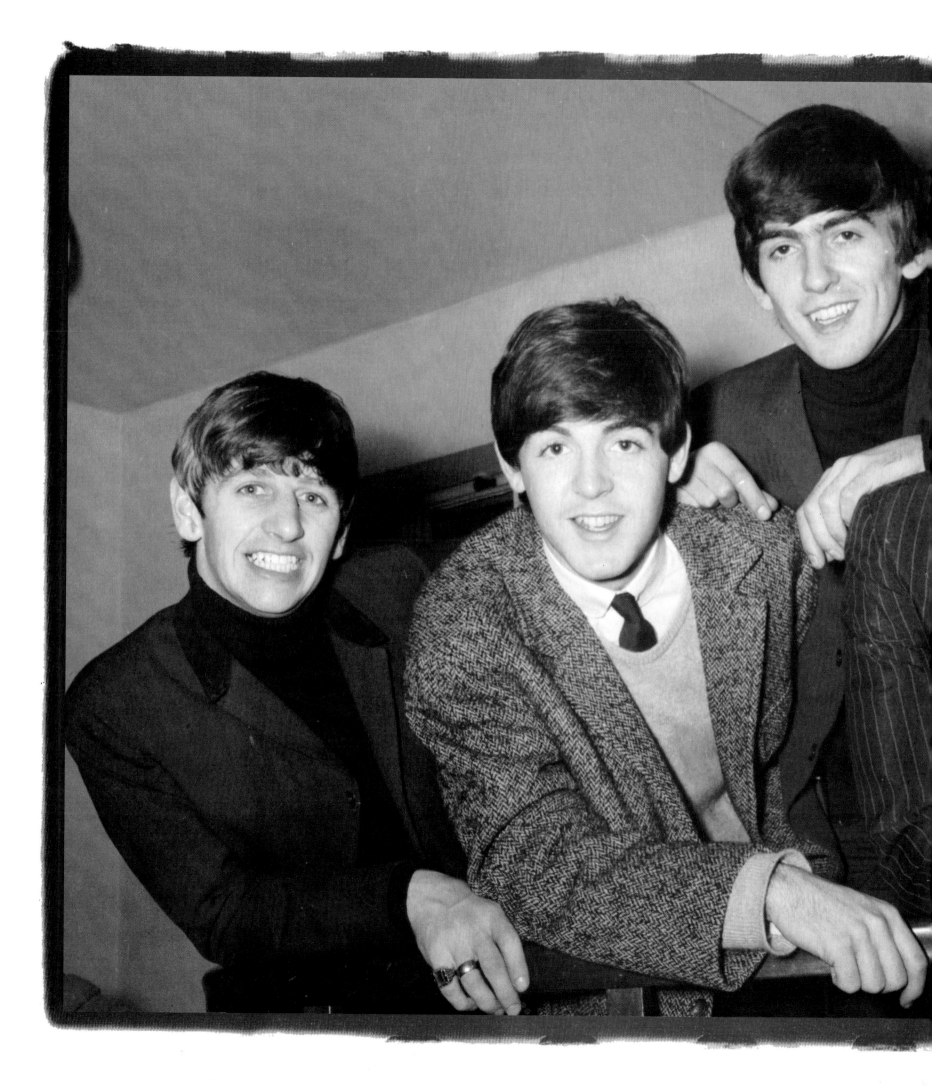

CHAPTER ONE

1963

IT WAS SUGGESTED THAT THE BEATLES were the "new youth", but Paul McCartney dismissed the idea. They were simply "now". Despite the tender age of their obsessive fans, the group themselves were obviously not adolescents; George Harrison was the youngest – and even he would soon be twenty-one. The passions they ignited seemed peculiar to pubescent infatuation, but it didn't stop there. They needed protection in order to play live, and yet even policemen asked for their autographs. Their fans were likened at first to those of Frank Sinatra when he appeared in Britain in 1942, and of Johnny Ray in 1955. But while promoters rubbed their hands with glee at each sell-out show, and the hysteria developed into full-scale Beatlemania, these same fans were dismissed by some as "morons" and "semi-savages". Pupils were given lines with the correct spelling of "beetles"; girls were expelled for skipping school to join ticket queues; and boys suspended for letting their short-backs-and-sides loll into "tea-cosy" moptops. A navy commander noted with alarm an "increased number of peculiar haircuts affected by teenaged members of the ship's company"; and in the cotton mills, screaming seamstresses walked out on strike when their persistent "yeah, yeah, yeahs" drove the boss to turn off the factory radio. The Beatles were suddenly everywhere – as ebullient as their fans were exuberant; as effortlessly expressive as their music was exhilarating. And the immensity of their fame soon eclipsed any sour hints of infamy when the country's cream joined the lobby to welcome them as ambassadors of the future. The Queen Mother spoke of them warmly. So did Edward Heath. So did Field Marshal Lord Montgomery. The "guitar-twanging gladiators from Liverpool" came, saw and conquered, with the only opposition coming from the "squares".

> "They are the most talented and primitive young men I have ever met. They are the voice of youth."
>
> **NORMAN PARKINSON,** PHOTOGRAPHER

"Ours is a today image."

IN THE DAYS before national television and radio embraced pop as one of its own, the newspapers wielded unprecedented power. In 1963 the BBC had yet to pit *Top Of The Pops* against *Thank Your Lucky Stars* and *Ready, Steady, Go!*, and Radio 1 was still years away from challenging Radio Luxembourg.

In print, the weekly *Melody Maker* and *New Musical Express* preached only to the converted, which left Fleet Street with the task of enlightening everyone else as to who was "in" and which sounds were "now".

The Beatles' ascent into the hallowed world of the dailies was painstaking. They had been professional since 1960 but needed to prove themselves with four No. 1s before the editors in London, traditionally disdainful of pop music, took notice. "It's taken a long time for the papers to realise that we've caught on", said Paul McCartney. "We knew a year ago we were catching on."

An early champion was the *Daily Mirror*'s Donald Zec who filed a two-page report on 10 September about the "Four frenzied Little Lord Fauntleroys who are making £5,000 [£58,000 today] every week". The Beatles were "cheeky-looking kids with stone-age hairstyles", he noted, "who knew their amps and ohms if not their Beethoven". They were "pleasing to look at, friendly of manner, and when one of them hollers 'Shurrup!', it is only a genial appeal for silence". Zec asked if they could read music. "No", said

John Lennon. "What do we want with that stuff anyway? It would interfere with our creations." Were they all alike? "You know the way people begin to look like their dogs?", answered John. "Well, we're beginning to look like each other."

For the national press as a whole, the watershed came on 13 October 1963 when The Beatles appeared on *Sunday Night At The London Palladium*. Bruce Forsyth was the host, Des O'Connor the big star, and "America's No. 1 balladeer" Brook Benton the special guest. But with their chart success preceding them, The Beatles topped the bill. They were on stage for just over ten minutes, into which they crammed four songs, ending with the orgiastic "Twist And Shout". But their between-song banter proved to be just as bewitching. They made fun of themselves, talked across each other and messed about as if they were back at the Cavern, not on prime-time TV. John Lennon slipped into his twisted-limb routine which, remarkably, seemed to offend no one. "Ours is a today image", he would go on to tell the papers. But to the screaming Palladium audience he merely cried out, "Shurrup!"

1963

■ The Beatles' first proper tour, a five-date visit to Scotland in January, grossed £210 [£2,450 today]. By November, they were commanding up to £800 [£9,300] for one half-hour show.

■ In January, they made their national TV debut with "Please Please Me" on ITV's *Thank Your Lucky Stars*.

■ In June, the BBC launched their own radio series, *Pop Go The Beatles*.

■ Their own magazine, *The Beatles Book Monthly*, began publication in August.

■ The same month, they appeared for the last time at the Cavern Club. (John first played there with The Quarry Men in 1957.)

■ When issued in America, "Please Please Me" peaked at No. 116.

■ By November, their second LP, *With The Beatles*, had received advance UK orders of 250,000 copies. For "I Want To Hold Your Hand" the figure was 1,000,000 copies.

■ Also that month, EMI's chairman Sir Joseph Lockwood announced that The Beatles' record sales so far that year had topped 3,000,000.

■ In December, a record twenty-two million viewers – more than one-third of the British population – watched all four Beatles on *Juke Box Jury*.

■ In *NME*'s end-of-year poll, The Beatles scooped 14,666 votes, almost as much as the other vocal groups put together. Just over 5,000 voted for Elvis.

■ In 1963 Beatles records grossed over £6,000,000 [£70,000,000].

Above and right: Four "cheeky-looking kids with stone-age hairstyles" and their *Daily Mirror* champion and critic Donald Zec, at his London flat in Maitland Court, Lancaster Terrace, on 9 September.

Facing page: John and Paul on stage – and all four off stage – at the Odeon Cinema, Cheltenham, Gloucestershire, on 1 November, the first date of their Autumn Tour.

The BEATLES Show TONIGHT
ALL TICKETS SOLD
NO TICKETS EXPECTED TO BE RETURNED
NO STANDING ROOM AVAILABLE

"Alarming, scream-filled torment."

THE PALLADIUM performance won the group degrees of praise in the following day's TV pages. In his *Daily Herald* column, the playwright Dennis Potter wrote: "The Beatles were undeniably entertaining in the furiously yobbish style now all the rave. I thought their showmanship was extremely accomplished. Drummer Ringo Starr held himself momentarily poised – deliberately condensing the excitement in a half-second of alarming, scream-filled torment." The *Daily Mirror*'s Clifford Davis was less certain: "They did nothing especially to excite their fans. Their singing and instrumental work wasn't particularly inspiring or provocative. And their movements, lacking all cohesion, production and polish, were remarkably restrained. Nothing calculated here, just four kids with grins, having a ball."

"This is a bit frightening."

Regardless of the critique, what fuelled Fleet Street's imagination was the effect the group had on their growing army of fans. An inexplicable sense of imbalance had been simmering away in the provinces since the spring, spilling over into hysteria whenever The Beatles could be seen in person. And now here it was displayed on national TV. "Riot Night At The London Palladium", blazed a headline in the *Sketch*. "Beatles Flee In Fantastic Palladium TV Siege", revelled the *Daily Mirror*.

The reports revealed that during the afternoon's rehearsals, fifty girls had broken into the theatre via an emergency exit and attempted to rush the stage. Staff threatened them with the in-house firehose and Palladium manager David Wilmot was compelled to dial 999.

As the group attempted to leave the building after the show, 1,000 girls surged towards the stage door. They pummelled on policemen's backs, knocking off their helmets, before a small band finally broke through the 100-strong cordon of uniformed officers. "We never dreamed it would be like this", admitted Ringo. "They've gone mad over us before, but this is a bit frightening."

Above: "Litter with love for The Beatles" wrote the *Daily Mirror* on 15 September, noting the chocolate bars, flowers, empty fruit-juice cans and teddy bears thrown onto the stage. The venue was London's Royal Albert Hall, where The Beatles shared the bill with The Rolling Stones at the Great Pop Prom, a charity event organised by teen magazines *Marylin*, *Valentine* and *Roxy* in aid of the Printers' Pension Corporation.

Facing page, and right: The Beatles, Billy J. Kramer and Susan Maughan celebrate their success at Victoria Embankment Gardens, London, on 10 September. All were winners in the 1963 Variety Club of Great Britain Awards, held at the nearby Savoy Hotel. The Beatles won Best Vocal Record with "From Me To You", as voted for by readers of *Melody Maker*.

This unseemly display was "The New Madness" declared *Time* magazine. "Beatle Bedlam", proffered one tabloid. "Britain's Newest Neurosis", reckoned another. "Beatle Fever!" suggested the *Herald*. "Beatlemania!" decided the *Daily Mirror*. In The Beatles, Fleet Street had discovered an inexhaustible fountain of newsworthiness, and promptly championed them as if they were a four-man team of routine England goalscorers. "From that day on", said Tony Barrow, the group's press officer, "everything changed." Within weeks The Beatles were national property.

"They have frenzy all about them", wrote a journalist in the *Sunday Citizen*. "Noise, penetrating as a Mersey tug's toot. Noise, confident as a Lime Street drunk. Five girls to sort their fan mail. A PR man with three phones and smooth words." "They've not been moulded", added Barrow, smoothly. "They're the genuine thing. What they are today, they were three years ago. Talented. Long-lasting."

Even the *Financial Times* had an angle, reporting in November with authoritative breathlessness: "Gramophone records of The Beatles are in such phenomenal demand that all the production resources of Electrical Musical Industries are being marshalled to meet mounting orders superimposed on factories already working to capacity to meet peak seasonal demand."

Which, according to the *Daily Mail*, translated as 400,000 advance sales for the group's new LP, which "is going to be one huge smash hit whether or not it deserves to be". The report marvelled at the fact that "teenagers galore have ordered *With The Beatles* without even hearing it – the fans will play it until it's transparent". ■

This page: In the heart of Derbyshire's Peak District, reported the *Sunday Mirror* on 19 October: "The Beatles were involved in fantastic scenes at a dance last night. Dozens of teenage girls, in a crowd of 2,000, were dragged swooning onto the stage by police at Buxton. As The Beatles played the girls crushed around the stage. They toppled like nine-pins and had to be manhandled to safety. Dressing rooms became clearing stations. A police spokesman said, 'It was fantastic. We had to draft in fifty Specials to help'."

Facing page: At Yeadon Airport, West Yorkshire, on 3 November after a concert in Leeds. The Beatles were flying back to London to take part in the Royal Command Performance the following day.

Hysterical "Screamagers"

THE PALLADIUM PANDEMONIUM was repeated on 31 October when up to 20,000 "screamagers" lined the roof of the Queen's Building at London Airport to see The Beatles arrive back from a short tour of Sweden.

Never before had so many youngsters turned out to see so few do nothing in particular. A wave, even a glimpse of the fabulous four, was enough to incite palpitations and make the sixpence admission onto the roof garden well worthwhile.

Beatlemania was given a huge, sustainable boost the following day when The Beatles embarked upon their six-week Autumn Tour of the UK. The first date was in Cheltenham, Gloucestershire, a bastion of retired army officers and conservative English gentility. Gloucestershire's social and intellectual barriers withered as fans stood in anticipation in the rain, in jodhpurs and in jeans, chanting "We want The Beatles! We want The Beatles!" One student from the local Cheltenham Ladies College even joined the throng in her mortar board.

"The power of music is more potent than political power", warned a music therapist, after the scenes at Cheltenham turned "riotous". "Subjecting immature girls to long, strong doses of crude, coarse, often over-syncopated combinations of sound vibrations can, and obviously does, lead to loss of self-control and low-toned moral behaviour."

But even a potential loss of self-control was deemed a safer bet than a potential loss of life. This was especially true in the Yorkshire city of Leeds where, despite a bomb-scare, the police refused to evacuate the Odeon Cinema where The Beatles were due to play. It would be safer *not* to ask 2,500 hysterical fans to leave quietly by the nearest exit, they reasoned, correctly gambling on a hoax. ■

This page: On stage in front of the opulent drapery of the Savoy Cinema, Northampton, on 6 November, just two days after their Royal Variety Performance in the presence of the Queen Mother and Princess Margaret.

In an effort to avoid further scenes of Beatlemania, promoters at the Savoy drafted in recruits from the Young Farmers Association, whose "strong-arm" tactics succeeded in preventing fans from running riot.

Above and left: The Beatles and bobbies in Birmingham's Operation Beat-The-Beatlemania, pictured in an alley leading to the dressing rooms of the Hippodrome Theatre on 10 November. Prior to the show thousands of fans waited for their idols for ten hours in heavy rain. The group's black Austin Princess was late, having broken down on the M1. "We were given a tow by the RAC", explained George. "After repairs we drove to the police headquarters in Birmingham, where they told us to put the helmets on."

"You have to keep your stars way up and look for others at the same time."

BRIAN EPSTEIN

First among equals, The Beatles line up on 16 November in Brian Epstein's NEMS stable of stars. Top picture, from left to right: The Beatles; Gerry & the Pacemakers (Gerry Marsden, Freddie Marsden, Les Chadwick, Les McGuire); Brian Epstein (standing, and close-up); and Billy J. Kramer & the Dakotas (Robin McDonald, Mike Maxfield, Billy J, Ray Jones, Tony Mansfield).

Below: John shoots his own home movie from the stalls of the Ritz Cinema, Belfast, on 8 November. The Beatles only managed to enter the venue after 300 policemen forced a passage through the crowd of several thousand screaming fans outside. An earlier plan, in which support act Peter Jay & the Jaywalkers were to make a conspicuous entrance at the front of the Ritz while The Beatles sneaked in round the back disguised in Andy Capp flat caps, was scotched by the Commissioner of the Royal Ulster Constabulary. "The Beatles must be seen", he insisted.

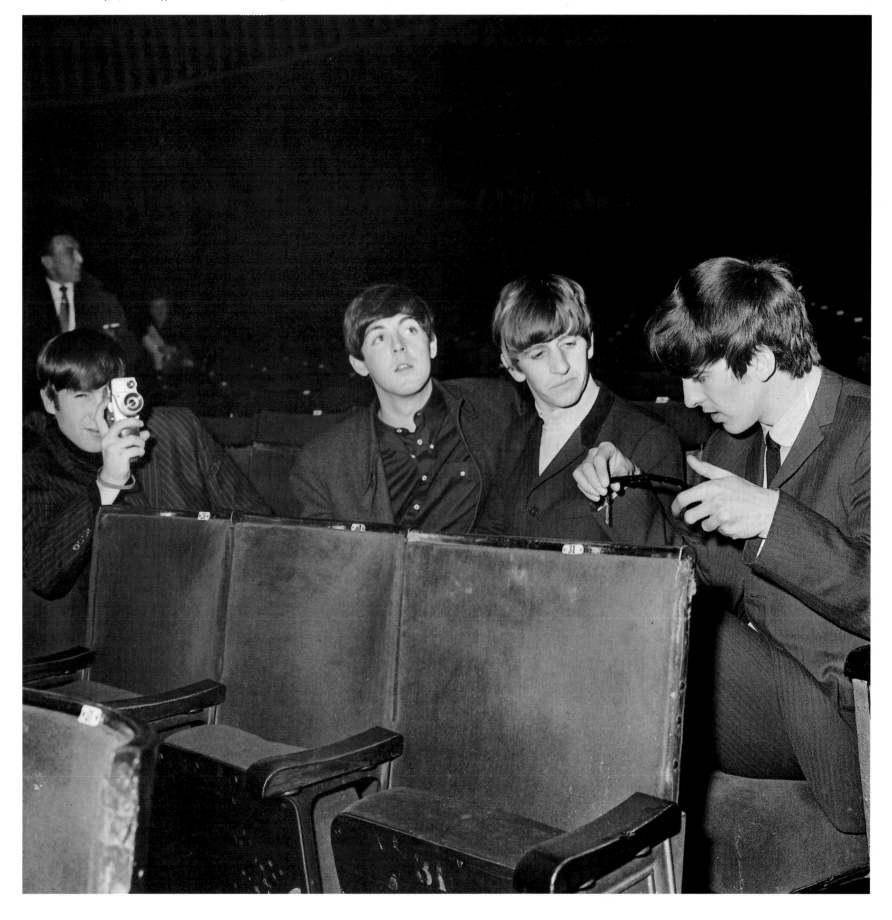

"If they press any harder, they'll come through as chips."

BOMBS ASIDE, the threat of rampaging teenagers was enough to prompt at least one promoter to cancel a planned concert on the grounds of security. "The time has come", he said, "when The Beatles will have to be brought into a hall in a cage, perform in a cage and leave in a cage." He wasn't far wrong. When they played a fan club show at the Palais in Wimbledon in December, the management placed the group on a makeshift platform enclosed behind a large steel mesh. But still the fans struggled to reach their idols. "If they press any harder", laughed Lennon, "they'll come through as chips."

Wimbledon saw the only actual cage, but to get in and out of venues with their "tea-cosy" hairstyles, their limbs and their dignities intact, The Beatles found themselves resorting to farcical disguises befitting props from a George Formby film. In Birmingham, the police hatched

Operation Beat-The-Beatlemania

Operation Beat-The-Beatlemania, in which the group were required to hide behind regulation overcoats and constables' helmets. Their "shaggy-dog" bowl cuts were combed into choirboys' quiffs in Sheffield; delivery-boy macs and an old yellow news van were deployed in Doncaster; while in Belfast the group were handed four brown flat caps in the style of Andy Capp (the *Daily Mirror*'s cartoon-strip, work-shy Northerner), until the commissioner of the Royal Ulster Constabulary banned the idea. "The fans must see The Beatles", it was decreed. "Otherwise there will be riots." Regardless of whether The Beatles could be seen or not, the riots continued. And as far as The Beatles were concerned, it wasn't just the fans who were getting carried away – the authorities were too. "We didn't really need the police helmets", George said of the Birmingham operation, which turned out to be more of a publicity stunt than a genuine attempt at security. "But it was great fun just the same. I think the police enjoyed it too."

Above: The Beatles pictured in Portsmouth on 12 November prior to a concert at the Guildhall. Despite the cheery faces, they disappointed thousands of fans by postponing the show until December due to Paul McCartney's gastric flu.

Facing page: On stage and in the stalls before the show at the Ritz Cinema, Belfast, on 8 November. On his way out of the venue, a delighted Paul receives an appreciative peck from Audrey Gowar, seventeen-year-old secretary of the Irish Beatles Fan Club.

Right: At the Granada Cinema, East Ham, on 9 November, the eighth night of their tour. George Martin visited The Beatles in their dressing room afterwards to tell them that advance sales of "I Want To Hold Your Hand", to be issued on 29 November, were approaching the one-million mark.

"They're at it again! Other countries have industrial riots, army revolts. Britain has Beatles drives."

DAILY MIRROR

Above and right: Between performances at the Coventry Theatre, Coventry, on 17 November, The Beatles race toy Scalextric cars on thirty feet of track set up in a backstage bar. "It's good fun and helps keep us relaxed", reckoned Ringo.

Above: Sober on the sofa at the City Hall, Newcastle, on 23 November.

Left: George takes a mystery girl out to dinner in London. "Her name is Hush-Hush and she's a friend of the family", he told reporters. Refusing to reveal her identity, he added: "As you will probably guess from her name, she's Chinese."

Facing page: The Beatles backstage at the Gaumont Cinema, Bradford, on 21 December. "They have remained cheerfully sane in front of the distorted mirror of insanity", observed the *Daily Sketch*.

Above: "Is it the sixth form of a self-consciously progressive comprehensive school?" asked the *Daily Mail* on 15 December. "Is it a bus outing to Blackpool? Nothing so jolly. It's the Mersey Sound. It is one of the most expensive line-ups of pop talent ever concentrated into one small area at one time." Which actually meant it was the cast of the all-Merseyside edition of *Thank Your Lucky Stars*, photographed at ABC's Alpha Television Studios, Aston Cross, Birmingham. From the left: Billy J. Kramer & the Dakotas, The Beatles, Cilla Black, and The Searchers (Chris Curtis, Mike Pender, Tony Jackson and John McNally). "With the lads and lasses of Liverpool", said host Brian Matthew, "anything can happen. It's simply one long laugh from beginning to end."

"I'm changing the concept of the pantomime."

THE BEATLES' appearance on *Sunday Night At The London Palladium* would prove to be as significant here as their *Ed Sullivan Show* debut would be the following February in the United States. Despite this, and the continuing onslaught of Beatlemania, their longevity was far from guaranteed; even John Lennon gave the group just five years. "The future of groups is extremely shaky", warned BBC Light Entertainment boss Jim Casey. "Unlike solo performers, what can groups do when the beat craze is over?"

But as the year drew to a close, the beat-boom showed no signs of waning. Liverpool became the subject of its own BBC documentary, *The Mersey Sound* – even if, according to the *Daily Mirror*, this "didn't really prove anything, except that The Beatles have something quite different from all the other groups".

Elsewhere, they topped the bill on the second all-Liverpool edition of ABC's prime-time *Thank Your Lucky Stars*, and created a tumultuous impact at the Royal Variety Performance, where

Something Quite Different

John invited the Queen Mother, and everyone else in a 20-guinea-seat, to rattle her jewellery in tune to "Twist And Shout".

The Beatles ended the year with their show at the Finsbury Park Astoria, which ran twice-nightly from Christmas Eve until mid-January 1964. The show was more of a revue than a concert and included support slots from Cilla Black and Rolf Harris. Not content with Beatlemania, manager Brian Epstein attempted to broaden the group's appeal yet further by hiring Peter Yolland, who conceived a script featuring corny lines and silly costumes.

"The new youth" or not, The Beatles still found themselves pandering to the demands of old-fashioned light entertainment, thanks largely to the efforts of Yolland, who had spent his career producing *Jack and Jill*, *Humpty Dumpty* and *Cinderella*. "I consider this a splendid challenge", he said in his own defence as he surveyed the show's giant snowman prop. The Beatles might be new, but he promised yet more novelty: "I'm changing the concept of the pantomime." ∎

Above: The Beatles on the set of their *Christmas Show* on 20 December at the 3,000-seat Astoria Cinema, Finsbury Park, London. Producer Peter Yolland told reporters: "I've worked in show business since 1948 but this will be the first time I've worked in a theatre with policemen trying to keep people out of it."

Left: Hostess Sheila Whitworth fastens Ringo's safety belt on a Viking aircraft. Brian Epstein paid £400 [£4,600] to charter the plane on Boxing Day to fly Ringo, Cilla Black, Tommy Quickly, and members of The Fourmost and the Dakotas from Liverpool, where they'd spent Christmas, back to London for further performances of *The Beatles' Christmas Show*. Also on board was Beatles' roadie Mal Evans.

CHAPTER TWO

1964

AT HOME, THE FRENZIED NATURE OF The Beatles' airport receptions prompted the Ministry of Aviation to reconsider arrangements for arrivals "of this kind". Abroad, France shunned them, America was twice entertained by them, while Denmark, Holland, Hong Kong, New Zealand and Australia embraced them like biblical heroes dispensing love and free money wherever they roamed.

"I am very fond of their programmes", murmured Labour leader Harold Wilson. In the Commons, Conservative Prime Minister Sir Alec Douglas-Home claimed responsibility for their success, prompting Wilson to declare, "Is nothing sacred?" In the City, Barclays Bank reported that they had become an "invisible export", which had made a "significant contribution towards the British balance of payments". US President Lyndon Johnson was similarly impressed. "I like your advance party", he told Sir Alec on a Washington visit (delayed a day to avoid a Beatles concert there), "but don't you think they need haircuts?"

> **"The most devastating male quartet since the Four Horsemen of the Apocalypse."**
>
> **DONALD ZEC, *DAILY MIRROR***

"The Beatles herald a cultural movement which may become part of the history of our time", predicted William Deedes, Minister Without Portfolio. And of other times, too, it seemed: those infamous hairstyles were discovered to be similar to those depicted in Caravaggio's masterpiece, *The Musicians*, painted in the sixteenth century. And in Clyde, New York, workmen demolishing a Victorian-era building discovered a mysterious card printed in 1878 announcing a dance by "The Beatles Full Orchestra".

Back in the present, The Beatles continued to scale new heights. "These boys are giants!", proclaimed a Capitol Records spokesman, chewing on his cigar. "No record, not even a Presley disc, has gone so far so fast as 'I Want To Hold Your Hand'." ■

"Fogbound" in France

THERE WAS REASON to believe The Beatles might not be as popular abroad as they were at home. Sweden had already succumbed to their effortless advance, but France promised to be more of a challenge.

"IT'S LIKELY to be their biggest test to date", warned the *Daily Mirror*, "for they are almost totally unknown in France." The local newspapers explained who The Beatles were. "They are a mad, mad bunch", wrote one. "Life in Britain today is completely based on these four gentleman singers. Everything in Britain goes on to a Beatle musical background." Others weren't so kind: "Ringo Starr is the ugliest of the lot. He is the drummer. He is 23. He has a big nose, big mouth and hooded eyes under his frightful fringe of hair – but everyone loves him."

The group arrived at Le Bourget Airport on 14 January to a quiet reception from about sixty fans. Large-scale curiosity was confined to the media, who outnumbered the fans two-to-one, and who followed the group via motorcade to Paris's exclusive George V hotel, where an even larger contingent thronged in the opulent foyer. Even Brigitte Bardot couldn't attract so many photographers, said a hotel barman.

Despite the media turnout, there were only three Beatles on display. Ringo remained in

Liverpool with his parents, privately reluctant to join the others, publicly "fogbound". Making the most of his late arrival, the group's new press officer Brian Sommerville promoted a deal with British European Airways, in which Ringo was photographed on the steps of a plane holding a "TLES" sign up to the airline's trademark "BEA". In return for the publicity, which also required the group to display their "BEAtles" flight bags as often as possible for the benefit of the cameras, the Liverpool entourage was granted unlimited flying between London and Paris – which compensated for their paltry French fee, scarcely sufficient to cover their expenses.

The Beatles were booked to play a three-week, two-shows-a-day residency at the Olympia Theatre in Paris, on a ten-act bill which also starred local chanteuse Sylvie Vartan, the American singer Trini "If I Had A Hammer" Lopez plus a number of jugglers and acrobats. "Les Beatles" were the official headliners, but Vartan and Lopez were received as the stars by the fans, the promoters and the French media. ∎

1964

■ In January, *Meet The Beatles*, the US version of *With The Beatles*, became the fastest-selling LP in American history.

■ Some 50,000 tickets were requested for The Beatles' US TV debut on the *Ed Sullivan Show* in February. The TV studio seated 728.

■ The same month, the *Wall Street Journal* estimated that $50 million [£17,900,000 then/£202,000,000 today] will be spent on Beatles' goods in the US alone in 1964.

■ In the 4 April issue of the music industry journal *Billboard*, The Beatles occupied the Top 5 singles in the Hot 100. The following week, they had fourteen

songs on the chart. Sales of Beatles' singles made up 60 per cent of the market, said the magazine.

■ 87 per cent of all dollars spent by US teenagers on records in 1964 went on The Beatles.

■ In the UK, a company called Musical & Plastic Industries Ltd reported a first-quarter rise in profits of £112,000 [£1,270,000] as sales of their toy Beatles guitars rose to 120,000 units per month.

■ More than one-quarter of the population of Liverpool, some 220,000 people, turned out to see

The Beatles receive a civic reception to coincide with the Northern premiere of *A Hard Day's Night* in July.

■ It was announced that in 1963 and 1964, 104 of the hundreds of young girls who'd gone missing from home in Britain had turned up in Liverpool. Most were found at the Cavern Club.

■ Culminating in a show in Kansas City in September, their fee for a single US concert rose in six months from around $3,500 to $150,000 [£54,000].

■ When seventeen-year-old Elaine Jones wrote to a New York newspaper requesting a pen-pal interested in The Beatles, 4,000 replies were delivered to her home in Sevenoaks, Kent.

Above: Ringo arrives on 15 January and promotes BEA on the steps of a Vanguard jet. "Il est perdu dans le brouillard", said the French press.

Right: John and George light up in London before heading for Paris.

Facing page: Les Beatles at a press conference held upon arrival at Le Bourget Airport, France, on 14 January. (Inset: The Beatles fly out to Paris.)

"Mersey beaucoup."

TWO THOUSAND PEOPLE witnessed The Beatles' warm-up gig at the Cinèma Cyrano, Versailles, but it could have been just 200. More screams were heard during the Dracula films shown prior to the first performance. There were no orgasms, no knicker-wetting or hysterics. There were hardly any girls, and the group made little attempt to win over the audience of stolid garçons; barely attempting any French save for Lennon's "Je me lève à sept heures" ("I get up at seven") and "Mersey beaucoup". Only their versions of already popular yé-yé songs like "Twist And Shout" elicited much response.

The reception was similarly glacial on the opening night at the Olympia, where the audience of Paris socialites in full evening dress didn't even think to rattle their jewellery. The Beatles' amplifiers kept breaking down, and the consuming lack of enthusiasm enervated the group's performance. The only real excitement was the ugly fight which followed an attempt by photographers to gatecrash the dressing room. "Our biggest regret is that we didn't see it", John

"Il est le plus gear."

said afterwards. "In the old days at the Cavern in Liverpool, we'd have been in there, boots and knees and all."

Most French reviews dismissed The Beatles as delinquents and British has-beens. But there was some excitement to be found among the few female French fans. "Oh, Georges, tu es absolutement fab", fourteen-year-old Marie-France Giraud enthused to the *Daily Mirror*'s Peter Stephens. While fifteen-year-old Maryvonne Rached declared, "Moi, j'adore Paul. Il est le plus gear et le plus fab de tous" – which Stephens translated as: "I'm crazy about Paul. He is the gearest and most fab of all."

Not that The Beatles were that bothered. Returning to the hotel, a telegram informed them that, inside a week, their new single, "I Want To Hold Your Hand", had leapt from No. 43 in the US Cashbox charts to No. 1. No British artist had managed such a feat before: the most important audience in the world had buckled before The Beatles had even set foot on American soil. And, as The Beatles left Le Bourget to return home on 5 February, even their French support had begun to pick up. At least 100 fans saw them off. ■

Above: Sylvie Vartan shows them how it should be done, after *Le Figaro* complained that "The Beatles hold their guitars like watering cans".

Left, top of strip and facing page: Out and about on the Champs-Elysées on 15 January. Not exactly "swamped mid-champs", as the *Daily Express* reckoned. Or as the *Daily Mail* put it: "Exactly three girls asked for their autographs."

Far left, bottom of strip: Posing outside the exclusive George V hotel.

Right: "The reception, I think, can be described as politely enthusiastic", wrote the *Daily Mail* of The Beatles' opening night of their residency at the Paris Olympia on 16 January. "When they yell", added Ringo, "it's more like a cheer than a squeal."

Below: Les Beatles contemplate three long weeks at the Olympia – France's version of the Palladium – sharing a bill with acrobats and jugglers, and playing to an audience of all-too-affable filles and over-gracious garçons.

Above: Qu'ils sont fab? Posing with picture postcards in the shadow of the Arc de Triomphe.

Left: Ennui at the encore. Paris socialites get up and go as The Beatles play yet another song. "One hardened Beatle fan who crossed with them to Paris", wrote the *Sunday Telegraph*, "was a bit taken aback on finding he could actually hear the music and even snatches of the words above the noise from the audience."

Below: The Beatles and Brian Epstein return from Paris on 5 February, flying the British flag and seeking "airport asylum" after their French experience.

Beatle Day, USA!

AT FIRST IT LOOKED as if the US might follow the Paris model and resist the English interlopers. America was introduced to The Beatles via TV when a clip of "She Loves You" was shown on the prime-time *Jack Paar Show* in early January.

Like France, America was sceptical. *New York Times* critic Jack Gould denounced the group as a low-brow "Presley multiplied by four", while Paar himself decided that, "on this side of the Atlantic it is dated stuff". More vociferous was the *Chicago Tribune* which, alerted by the enthusiasm of a local radio station, warned its readers of the "Beatles menace". The British sound was just too square for American teenagers, presumed the pundits, and The Beatles were merely regurgitating white rock'n'roll and black R&B – even Cliff Richard said as much in the *Daily Mirror*. Capitol Records, EMI's outlet in the United States, had already pressed the point by turning down three previous Beatles singles, and watched them all flop when subsequently licensed to independents.

And yet, by 10 January, "I Want To Hold Your Hand" had sold a million copies in the US (when 200,000 meant a sure-fire hit), by which time American editors were despatching journalists to the George V hotel in Paris to find out exactly what this phenomenon known as "Beatles" was all about. The British papers, meanwhile, were indulging in a half-hearted backlash in the wake of the Dave Clark Five knocking "I Want To Hold Your Hand" off the UK No. 1 spot. The "Tottenham Sound" was where it was at now, they said.

As Britain scoffed, America held its breath, waiting for The Beatles' arrival. "New York police are bracing themselves for a battle", wrote the *Observer*'s correspondent in the city, Evelyn Irons. "The Beatles arrive at Kennedy Airport at 1.40 p.m. next Friday and their promoters expect the wildest fan scenes since Elvis Presley's heyday."

"A nervous excitement is running through American life as Beatle Day draws near", agreed the *Herald*'s man in New York, John Sampson. "The group arrive on Friday, heralded by an outbreak of Beatle wigs, Beatle buttons, Beatle hats, Beatle pillows, Beatle haircuts. There are even Beatle clubs." ∎

Top: At New York City's newly named John F. Kennedy Airport on 7 February with their promotional BEA-tles flight bags and rival luggage courtesy of Pan Am.

Left: With show host Ed Sullivan on 8 February. "I've seen nothing like it", he said, "and that includes Elvis Presley's three appearances in 1958."

Facing page: A CBS photocall before the *Ed Sullivan Show.*

Bottom: From left to right: Ringo, ever the keen photographer, at the New York press conference given upon The Beatles' arrival; John and Cynthia at the airport, and on a train to Washington, DC, on 11 February – Cynthia is wearing a dark wig over her blonde hair; and George with his sister Louise, who had emigrated to the United States a decade earlier and released her own "speaking album" reminiscing about the Harrisons' childhood days together in Liverpool.

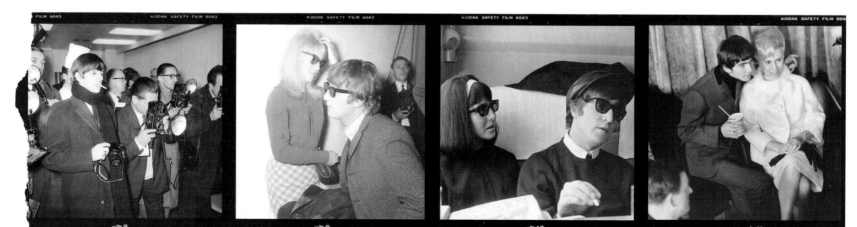

"The temperature is 32 Beatle degrees."

THE BEATLES flew out to America on 7 February for a promotional visit lasting two weeks, which included three live appearances on the coast-to-coast *Ed Sullivan Show*, two showcase concerts, endless rounds of interviews and a week spent at Miami Beach.

While they wondered aloud on board the plane why America should even be interested, the group's arrival was being anticipated by radio broadcasts such as New York City's WMCA: "It is now 6.30 a.m., Beatle time. They left London thirty minutes ago. They're out over the Atlantic Ocean, headed for New York. The temperature is 32 Beatle degrees."

At the newly named John F. Kennedy Airport, the sound of jet engines was drowned by the shrill shrieks of more than 5,000 screamagers, whose presence, the sceptics said, was prompted by a radio giveaway of a T-shirt and a dollar bill.

"There won't be many there", said Ringo.

But the hysteria was real enough. "Don't wave or smile", The Beatles were warned, "the fans can barely contain themselves just looking at you." That much couldn't be denied. The screams reached a new crescendo at every stage of the arrival – as the plane came into view. As it landed. As it taxied across the runway. As the doors opened. As The Beatles stepped out. As their guitar cases appeared on a luggage trolley.

"They told us it would be fab", wrote George Harrison in his *Daily Express* column the following day. "But this was ridiculous! We have seen some mobs of fans in our time but somehow we weren't prepared for what was waiting for us. 'There won't be many there', said Ringo. 'The airport's too far out from the city.' Was he wrong!"

Even seasoned American newsmen appeared overwhelmed by the scene. One reporter began dictating his story with the words, "Not since the day General MacArthur returned from Korea . . ." Back in the UK, the group's fans were just as transfixed: it was later reported that one-fifth of the entire population had tuned into the BBC's *Saturday Club* to hear a minute-by-minute account of the reception. ■

Above: The Beatles rehearse their appearance on the *Ed Sullivan Show* at CBS TV's Studio 50 in Manhattan, New York City. "Please!", said Sullivan to the hysterical studio audience during the live broadcast the following day, "I must remind you that there are other great stars on this stage". He was clearly taken aback, as was Frank Sinatra, whom George quoted in his *Express* column. "I thought The Beatles would die in New York", said Ol' Blue Eyes. "I was surprised by the reception they got. I was wrong." Another of America's biggest stars extended an offer of friendship to the opposition, but at least one of The Beatles was having none of it. After being told that they'd been sent a cable of congratulations from Elvis, George asked: "Elvis who?"

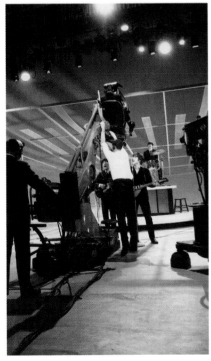

This page: Rehearsing for the *Ed Sullivan Show* on 9 February with roadie Neil Aspinall standing in for a bed-ridden George. The same evening The Beatles played live in front of the biggest TV audience America had ever seen, most of which undoubtedly agreed with fifteen-year-old Regina Kaye, whose reaction was reported the following day. "Their singing tears me apart and lets out all the frustration", she said. "It just kills you." Her enthusiasm wasn't shared by the nation's cultural commentators, least of all the blustery *New York Times*, which wrote: "The Beatles' vocal quality can be described as hoarsely incoherent with the minimal enunciation necessary to communicate the schematic texts."

Great performers

THE BEATLES were bustled into a press conference upon arrival at JFK, where they quickly won over the 200 largely combative members of the US media who'd been set on exposing them as an English gimmick. Do you come from a show business background? asked a reporter. "Well, my dad used to say me mother was a great performer", replied John.

Film, TV and stills cameras peered into their faces, while all sizes and ranges of microphone captured precious seconds of Beatle conversation. Within days, spoken-word LPs were raking in unauthorized dollars and Beatle wigs were being manufactured at a rate of 35,000 per day.

Astonished by their humour and the continued success of their records, the US media immediately took The Beatles to heart. As George was confined to bed with a throat infection, Maureen Cleave wrote in the *Evening Standard*, "America gets madder, crazier, wilder about our Beatles every second. Coast to coast yesterday the news was 'Beatle has bug'. George's 'strep' throat came first, Cuba, Cyprus, etc., came after".

> **"So this is America!", said Ringo in the midst of it all. "They all seem out of their minds."**

On 9 February, at the CBS Studios in New York, nearly 730 teenagers screamed as The Beatles made their debut on the *Ed Sullivan Show*. In the outside world, 100,000 times that number – an estimated seventy-three million – watched it all on TV. The crime rate plummeted as America's biggest-ever audience stayed in to see what Donald Zec referred to as "the most devastating male quartet since the Four Horsemen of the Apocalypse".

A full-blown American tour was planned for the summer, but for now The Beatles played just three concerts, one at the Washington Coliseum and two at New York's Carnegie Hall. The Coliseum was memorable for its ludicrous revolving stage, which saw Ringo rocking on his rickety drum riser and The Beatles being rotated every few minutes so that they could be seen by fans in each corner of the arena. At the Carnegie Hall, demand for tickets was so great that seats were placed on stage with the group, among them the wife of the New York State governor, Mrs Nelson Rockefeller. Just 5 per cent of the audience were adults.

Above: Being harassed by the local wildlife on 14 February, St. Valentine's Day, at Miami Beach, Florida, where they made a second *Ed Sullivan Show* appearance two days later.

Facing page, top: On the *Ed Sullivan Show* in New York.

Facing page, bottom: "It's hotter than it is at Blackpool on an August Bank Holiday", said Ringo as The Beatles cruised off the coast of Miami Beach on the ninety-three-foot luxury yacht *Southern Trail*.

Below: A photo-opportunity at the New York press conference a week earlier.

"I know we've hit it big . . ."

GEORGE HARRISON, the youngest Beatle, came of age on 25 February 1964. He received fifty-two sacks of mail, containing an estimated 15,000 birthday cards from fans all over the world. Most were delivered to EMI's head office in Manchester Square, London, where George and the club's beehived secretary Anne Collingham opened as many as they could before the novelty wore off. Two more van-loads arrived at George's parents' home in Hunts Cross, Liverpool, where his father Harold, a senior bus driver, took the day off work to help his wife and a neighbour deal with the avalanche of paper and parcels.

"I don't know where I am going to put them", said Mrs Louise Harrison, as three postmen unloaded half-a-dozen hampers crammed with teddy bears, records, electric razors, socks, shirts, hair brushes, shampoo by the gallon, and untold

> ## "I don't know if I'll ever be a millionaire."

boxes of jelly babies. One fan even sent a full-sized door which George was supposed to unlock with one of his hundreds of twenty-first ceremonial keys.

"I shall keep everything here until George comes up for the weekend", promised his mum, as The Beatles, having arrived back from their visit to the United States just three days before, began recording songs for their first film at EMI's studios in St. John's Wood. "I telephoned him to wish him a happy birthday soon after midnight, at the hour at which he was born. We sang to each other and had a good laugh."

Taking stock in the *Daily Mirror*, George was philosophical about The Beatles' success so far. "I don't think I've changed", he said, "I know we've hit it big, but I don't know if I'll ever be a millionaire. We get only two bob from every £1 we earn, and that's split four ways – sixpence each. If I miss anything in my life now, I don't know what it is, because we haven't got time, any of us, to think what we are missing."

He didn't have time to read much of the mail either and most remained unopened by early March when it was sent away to be pulped: "It could have gone to a children's hospital", complained a letter to the *Mirror*.

Above: George endures his twenty-first birthday on 25 February with The Beatles' Fan Club secretary Anne Collingham.

Left: Three postmen deliver two van-loads of cards and presents to George's parents at their home in Hunts Cross, Liverpool.

"I think they are lovely boys."

MARCH SAW THE BEATLES hob-nobbing with Britain's elite: with Labour leader Harold Wilson at the Dorchester Hotel on the nineteenth, and with the Duke of Edinburgh at the Empire Ballrooms, Leicester Square, central London, on the twenty-third of the month.

The leader of Her Majesty's Opposition demonstrated his famous "common touch" by hosting the twelfth annual Variety Club of Great Britain reception, at which The Beatles were named Showbusiness Personalities of 1963. Speaking as MP for Huyton, Merseyside (the constituency of Ringo's parents), Wilson deftly played the game he deplored, when he said: "We are all proud of the creation of a new musical idiom in world communications. But I will refrain from making political capital out of The Beatles, unlike the leader of a certain political party."

"These blokes are helping people to enjoy themselves."

The Labour leader's wife, Mary Wilson, was equally opportunistic in her support of the group: "I think they are lovely boys", she said. "Harold and I are both tremendous fans and always listen to them and watch them on television. I feel quite sentimental listening to their Liverpool accents because Harold and I met there. Even in those days we used the word 'gear', meaning fabulous or wonderful."

The Beatles met Prince Philip when he hosted the Carl-Alan Awards – the Oscars of the ballroom dancing world, sponsored by Mecca – where he presented them with honours for Best Group of 1963, and for Best Vocal Record ("She Loves You"). Although the Queen would later comment, "I like listening to The Beatles, but I don't like the screaming that goes with them", the Duke of Edinburgh had no such reservations. "I think it is entirely helpful", he said, when asked about Beatlemania. "I really could not care less how much noise people make. I would much rather they make any noise they like singing and dancing. What I object to is people fighting and stealing. It seems to me that these blokes are helping people to enjoy themselves, and that is far better than the other thing." ■

Above: George accompanies eighteen-year-old actress Hayley Mills to the midnight premiere of the comedy-thriller, *Charade*, at the Regal Theatre, Henley-on-Thames, on 19 March.

Right: "I'm very fond of your programme", Labour Party leader Harold Wilson tells Ringo at the Dorchester Hotel, where The Beatles receive Variety Club of Great Britain awards for 1963.

Below: The Duke of Edinburgh and "those blokes" help people to enjoy themselves at the Carl-Alan Awards, Empire Ballroom, Leicester Square, on 23 March.

TV Times

TV WAS BECOMING INCREASINGLY important for The Beatles. Although radio had snapped them up by offering them their own weekly series before the papers really took any notice, radio lacked the visceral thrill that came with visuals. Fans could already see The Beatles' pictures in the papers and on LP sleeves, and they could hear them on record, but TV made the experience that much more real – TV made them move.

The small-screen's two-pronged attack on the senses had already magnified The Beatles' appeal in both Britain and the United States. The ubiquity, yet relative novelty, of the medium also meant that millions of casual viewers found themselves exposed to the group's charms as they waited to see a Lionel Blair or Cab Calloway. But it worked both ways – their appearances on the *Ed Sullivan Show* had pushed the programme to No. 1 in the ratings for the first time in seven years. This fact, plus Brian Epstein's theatrical background, inspired an expansion of The Beatles' TV horizons far beyond those defining the average four-man beat band.

On 13 March, the *Daily Mirror*'s TV editor Clifford Davis revealed Brian's plan for a "Beatles Spectacular – a TV show of shows", which would complement the group's charisma with costumes and comedy. It would be screened in early May, he wrote, and then offered to American, French, German and other TV networks around the world. In financial terms, it could earn more than £250,000 [£2,830,000] for a £10,000 [£113,000] investment. . . "A normal TV spectacular, networked coast-to-coast in the USA, would bring in around £75,000 [£850,000]", Davis added. "It looks like being British TV's biggest-ever TV business coup."

In the meantime, regular pop shows like *Ready, Steady, Go!* and its BBC rival *Top Of The*

Pops were natural outlets, and later in the month The Beatles appeared on both, miming to "Can't Buy Me Love", "You Can't Do That", and on *Ready, Steady, Go!*, a third song, "It Won't Be Long".

Ready, Steady, Go! went out on the twentieth, just a few hours before the BBC screened *The Variety Club Awards* – it was "Beatles benefit night", groaned Neville Randall in the *Sketch*: "The credits at the end reminded me that we also got glimpses of other chart-topping singers, Dusty Springfield and Alma Cogan. The glimpses were brief. The girls were just the supporting cast last night. The cameras switched back as soon as they could to the four young men of the hour."

Neville wasn't that keen on The Beatles. The show, he said, was: "Half-an-hour of free plugs for the next Beatles record, the first Beatles film, and even the first Beatles book. Cathy McGowan asked Paul what he thought of America. After a decent interval she asked Ringo the same question. Keith Fordyce asked John to tell us about his book, written two years ago but not considered worth publishing until Tuesday."

His criticism was even-handed and he concluded his review with this appraisal of The Beatles' new single: "At the risk of infuriating every viewer under twenty, I must confess that I thought very little of 'You Can't Do That'. But 'Can't Buy Me Love' is a winner." ∎

Top left: *Ready, Steady, Go!* hostess Cathy McGowan grills Ringo, the most popular Beatle in America, about the group's recent, massively successful trip to the United States.

Left, inset and facing page: The weekend starts here, on 20 March, as the "four young men of the hour" hog the limelight on *Ready, Steady, Go!*, broadcast live from London.

Around The Beatles

BRIAN EPSTEIN'S TV show of shows was provisionally called *John, Paul, George and Ringo*, but was screened as *Around The Beatles*. The revised title was suggested by the format – the group appeared on a central stage with the audience surrounding them on all sides.

The hour-long programme was made by Associated-Rediffusion, the company responsible for *Ready, Steady, Go!*, and was recorded at the station's own Studio 5 in Wembley – the largest TV studio in the world, boasting 14,000 square feet and 680 lighting circuits. Only a small portion of these facilities was required for The Beatles' first TV spectacular, but Brian surely appreciated the superlative.

For their producer, The Beatles chose Jack Good – "the beat programme specialist" – who'd brought rock'n'roll to British viewers with his *6.5 Special* in 1957, and who'd gone on to make series like *Oh Boy!*, *Boy Meets Girls* and *Wham!*, before moving to America to oversee "fast-moving pop music shows" for US TV in the early sixties.

Good was an ideas man, and wasted no time persuading The Beatles, against their better judgement, to appear in a couple of spoof Shakespeare sketches in which they'd busk through the period prose decked out in Elizabethan fashions. For the introductory section, John, Paul and George were required to dress as heralds and hold up trumpets in a mock fanfare, while Ringo appeared as Sir Francis Drake, complete with cape, plumed hat, doublet and hose, to declare the show open by hoisting a flag and firing a small cannon. This was the signal for hordes of fans wielding Beatle-friendly banners to rush onto the stage with all the brashness of Beatlemania, but also with a definite dose of decorum. "Behave like ordinary people", Good instructed them, "not teenage monsters."

But the "500 largely leather-clad 'birds' in the audience" were indeed "like teenage monsters", observed the *Daily Mail*'s Barry Norman.

Later in the show, Good indulged his passion for the Bard further by having The Beatles act out a burlesque on the Interlude section of *A Midsummer Night's Dream*. "The boys will be seen in the play-within-the-play that Bottom and his friends perform", he said with obvious delight. John took the role of the heroine Thisbe, Paul played Bottom (who in turn played Pyramus), while George was Moonshine and Ringo became Lion. Completing the

cast was actor Trevor Peacock, who played Wall. "At rehearsals they have all had a good go at Shakespeare", said Good, oblivious to The Beatles' wariness, "and I think it will work out at fifty-fifty Beatles to Shakespeare in the final dialogue."

The theatrics were only set-pieces, and Brian was more rightly concerned about the music. "Until now, The Beatles have never sounded right on television", he told the *Daily Mirror*. "That is why we have had them miming on most of their appearances. But on this show, none of their record hits will be mimed." Which wasn't strictly true. Sure enough, they didn't mime to their records, but earlier they had re-recorded new versions of eleven songs for the Beatles-as-the-Beatles section of the programme, among them a never-repeated medley of all their singles to date – "Love Me Do", "Please Please Me", "From Me To You", "She Loves You" and "I Want To Hold Your Hand" – plus a riotous version of the Isley Brothers' "Shout". ∎

This page: The Beatles rehearse on 28 April for their first TV spectacular *Around The Beatles* **at Rediffusion's Wembley TV studios in London. "Zounds! It's enough to make Will Shakespeare twist and shout in his grave", wrote the** *Daily Mirror.*

Facing page and overleaf: With guests such as PJ Proby, the Vernons Girls, Long John Baldry, Millie, US dance group the Jets, the Epstein-managed acts Cilla Black and Sounds Incorporated, and even a cameo by New York DJ and self-styled "Fifth Beatle" Murray The K, *Around The Beatles* was declared an unequivocal hit. "It was noisy and brash", wrote Clifford Davis in the *Daily Mirror*. "But it was glossy, slick and professional. It burst out of the screen. None of our pop music shows, on either channel, will be the same after this."

"We want a quiet holiday."

JOHN LENNON

Two Beatles compete at croquet and battle it out in the grounds of Dromoland Castle Hotel with swords from a suit of armour found in the castle's hall. John and George, along with Cynthia Lennon and Pattie Boyd, spent an Easter weekend in the luxury hotel in County Clare, Ireland, away from the fans. "We don't want people to know we're here", said John. "We want a quiet holiday."

Reunion Drinks in the Theatre Bar

IN MAY AND JUNE 1964, Brian Epstein expanded his NEMS operations by booking the Prince of Wales Theatre in London, where The Beatles had scored so spectacularly at the Royal Command Performance six months before, for a series of seven Sunday concerts billed as *Pops Alive!*

Introduced by DJ Alan Freeman, the shows starred NEMS' most popular acts, Billy J. Kramer & the Dakotas and Gerry & the Pacemakers, plus chart regulars like Dusty Springfield and Roy Orbison. The Beatles' two performances on 31 May were their first for a month (they'd spent the previous four weeks on separate, long-haul holidays). Their return to the London stage was deemed newsworthy enough to require a press conference beforehand, and a photo-call during which "the singers shared reunion drinks in the theatre bar". The following day, Beatlemania was still as indomitable as ever, the *Daily Mirror* was happy to report. Police reinforcements had to be called as 300 ticketless teenagers tried to storm the side entrance to the theatre. Inside, twelve girls collapsed during the two shows; one was carried out in a fit of hysterics and sped to Charing Cross Hospital in an ambulance. Such continued episodes led certain academics to ponder the power of The Beatles' prowess. According to Dr William Sargant, of the department of psychological medicine at St. Thomas' Hospital, London, the pattern was clear. The group were able to "produce trance states in some teenagers similar to those induced by voodoo or witch-doctors", he said. ∎

Left, inset (above) and facing page, top: Back together again, The Beatles busk it as barmen, toasting their "reunion" in the Saloon Bar at the Prince of Wales Theatre in London on 31 May after a month away from the stage.

Below: George and his new girlfriend Pattie Boyd and Ringo and Hayley Mills at the Pickwick Club in London's West End, at a party thrown on 8 April in honour of the Oscar-winning actor Anthony Newley and his wife Joan Collins, who recently returned to the UK from the States.

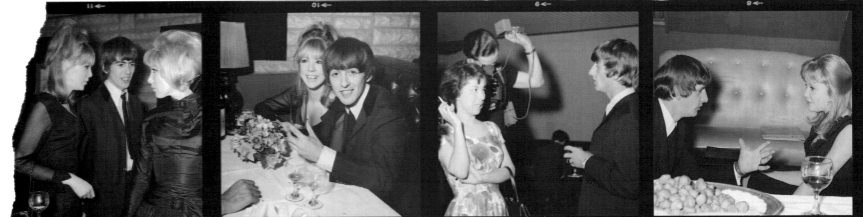

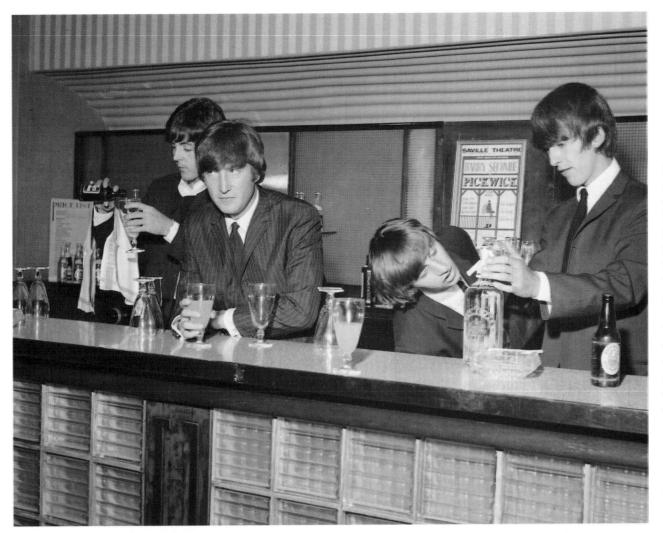

"Not so brite?"

IN APRIL, to celebrate the publication of *In His Own Write*, John was invited to a literary luncheon at the Dorchester Hotel, organised by London booksellers Foyle's. But to cries of "Shame!", the luncheon's chairman, cartoonist Osbert Lancaster, announced to guests that the Beatle "firmly refuses to get up and address you himself". To which John did briefly rise to his feet to say, "Thank you very much, God bless you".

"It was disappointing", admitted hostess Christina Foyle, "but he is very young." As John explained afterwards, "Speechmaking isn't my line of country. I would be embarrassed". Brian Epstein stepped in on his behalf, adding, "John Lennon is a wonderfully engaging companion, full of brain and charm and wit, all three of which he seeks unsuccessfully to conceal. For he is also a shy man".

Another ally was Lord Chandos, described by the *Sunday Telegraph* as "an inveterate and skilled after-dinner speaker", and by himself as "an old square". In a letter to Lennon sent in June, the peer wrote, "The freedom of speech in which we all believe must be matched, in a civilised society, by the freedom of silence".

"Full of brain and charm and wit."

Over in the House of Commons, Tory MP Charles Curran attacked John not for his inability to speak, but for his apparent inability to write. Opening a debate on education, he referred to John as "almost the most celebrated living Englishman", but denounced him for being "in a state of pathetic near-illiteracy".

Quoting the story "Deaf Ted, Danoota, (and me)" from a copy of *In His Own Write*, Curran said: "This boy seems to be a sort of throw-back from HG Wells' *Mr Polly* – and Mr Polly went to school nearly 100 years ago. He seems to have picked up bits of Tennyson, Browning and Robert Louis Stevenson while listening with one ear to the football results."

Speaking from Sydney, Australia, where The Beatles were on tour, John replied: "If Mr Curran thinks I'm illiterate he should have a look at a few other people my age. My writing was just a hobby. Someone asked me to put it together into a book. I've had as good an education as anybody else. It was just boring, that's all." ▪

Above: The finger points at John Lennon who, according to the *Daily Mail*, "did not want to speech" at a luncheon celebrating the publication of *In His Own Write*. It was "very feeble" and "a poor show", denounced Sir Alan Herbert, after noting that 3,000 people had applied for the luncheon's tickets – Foyle's biggest literary attraction since George Bernard Shaw.

Left: The Big O opens wide for John and Ringo at a Soho party to celebrate his twenty-eighth birthday on 23 April. Roy's wife Claudette was the host, and the Orbisons' eldest son, six-year-old Roy Jnr, mingled with the stars.

"The Beatles netted almost as many

votes as all the other groups combined."

NEW MUSICAL EXPRESS

The Beatles top the bill at the twelfth annual *NME* Poll Winners' All-Star Concert at the Empire Pool Wembley on 26 April in front of "20,000 screaming, shaking, twisting fans". The afternoon show took place just after the completion of *A Hard Day's Night* and in the midst of rehearsals for *Around The Beatles*. They arrived at the venue in a catering lorry escorted by police motorcyclists, and spent just over ten minutes on stage, rattling through a set featuring "She Loves You", "You Can't Do That", "Twist And Shout", "Long Tall Sally" and "Can't Buy Me Love".

"I've never seen them in the flesh."

A FLURRY OF ARTISTIC activity surrounded The Beatles in April and May. They featured in three canvases in the Royal Academy's summer exhibition, in two elsewhere and were sculpted in two entirely different media.

Royal Academician Ruskin Spear included a Beatles' photo in his painting *Sherry Bar Portrait*, which depicted a barmaid at his local in Chiswick. Deaf-and-dumb artist Alfred Thompson from Chelsea painted their picture as an offering of thanks – "For the Beatles gave him his first sound of music, through his hearing aid", explained the *Daily Mirror*. "My husband has been deaf all his life", Mrs Gertrude Thomspon added. "We tried to make him listen to other kinds of music but The Beatles were the first he could hear properly. He was absolutely thrilled."

Ringo, meanwhile, was featured in a "pop" portrait of twenty-year-old Gillian Brooke by her boyfriend Barry Fantoni. "The picture is supposed to show Gillian's likes and dislikes", said the artist. "She's crazy about Ringo and thinks I am a bit like him."

Their "likenesses" were also included in an abstract work by Egyptian-born painter Amal Matouk – "I've never seen them in the flesh", she explained; and in a futuristic work by Laurence Isherwood, whose *Beatles-in-the-year-2024* portrait was included in his seventy-fifth one-man show in London. "I've painted them with Beatle fringes, bald heads, red noses and I've given Paul just one tooth", he said, apparently straight-faced.

Elsewhere leading sculptor David Wynne forged their features in a £1,500 [£17,000], four-bust bronze; while for the man-in-the-street, Madame Tussaud's Waxworks museum in London unveiled their 1963-styled, life-sized effigies at a press conference attended by the real-life Lennon, McCartney, Harrison and Starr. Within a year, Tussaud's would announce a £34,000 [£385,000] rise in profits, thanks largely to The Beatles. ■

Left and above: Life-sized idols. Brand new but already a year out of date, on 29 April the real-life Beatles unveil plaster-of-paris and wax models based on their 1963 selves at Madame Tussaud's in London's Baker Street, having attended a glass-eye-matching session on the set of *A Hard Day's Night* back on 12 March. When the dummies were flown to Canada in July, for an exhibition in Vancouver, squealing girls kissed them as they were unloaded, while others tried to snip off locks of hair.

Back-up Beatle
from Barnes

ON 3 JUNE, The Beatles were at a photographic studio in Barnes, southwest London, posing for the US magazine *Saturday Evening Post*, when a potential disaster struck: Ringo collapsed, suffering from tonsillitis. To confound matters, he also had pharyngitis, an infection of the throat, and was rushed to hospital. The group's first world tour, visiting Denmark, Hong Kong, Australia and New Zealand, was due to begin the next day, and with Beatlemania as rampant in Copenhagen as it was in Kowloon and Queensland, not a single date could be cancelled.

A temporary drummer was found in Jimmy Nicol, "a musician from the background of pop", as the *Daily Express* put it, who lived, of all places, in Barnes and whose pedigree was impeccable. He'd previously recorded with Cliff Richard and Billy Fury, and he'd joined Georgie Fame and the Blue Flames just the week before.

"A musician from the background of pop."

"I'm knocked out, man", admitted the stand-in drummer, who was relaxing in an armchair after lunch when George Martin rang to offer him the job. "It's all hit me so suddenly."

Following a three-hour rehearsal of the Beatles' six-song live set at EMI's studios in Abbey Road that day, John, Paul, George and Jimmy flew out to Denmark for two shows on the fourth, while Ringo languished in a hospital in Bloomsbury, London.

Ringo wasn't fit enough to work again for another week, after which he was discharged and flew from London Airport (travelling on the same plane as actress Vivien Leigh) to join the rest of the group in Australia for a concert on the fifteenth.

After a reunion press conference in Melbourne, during which The Beatles were momentarily a five-man band with two drummers, Jimmy Nicol was returned to the background of pop with a fee of £500 [£5,600], plus expenses, and a gold Eternamatic watch engraved with the words: "From The Beatles and Brian Epstein to Jimmy – with appreciation and gratitude." ∎

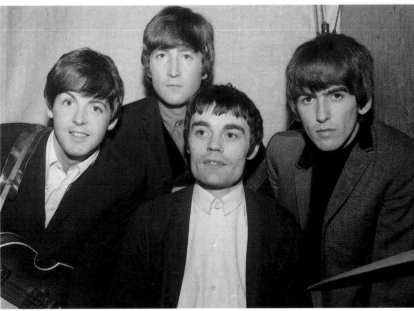

Right: George looks glum as "Jimmy the Cockney" is brought in at a moment's notice to replace an ailing Ringo on The Beatles' forthcoming world tour. "I'm knocked out, man", admitted the stand-in drummer, who was relaxing in an armchair after lunch when George Martin rang to offer him the job. "It's all hit me so suddenly."

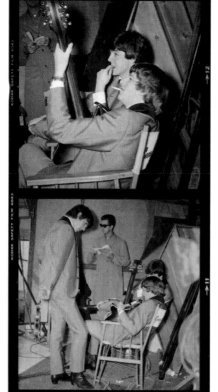

"It's THAT film with THOSE boys!"

THE LONDON PREMIERE of *A Hard Day's Night* on 6 July was a well-behaved riot of idolatry. Both public and press fell over themselves to worship The Beatles. Every seat in the 1,186-capacity Pavilion cinema in Piccadilly Circus had been sold in minutes, while one thousand times that number of fans stood outside in the summer heat, screaming and chanting.

Inside, Princess Margaret and her husband Anthony Armstrong-Jones grinned in full evening dress, while chatting with the film's stars. Paul said the group's recent trip to Australia had been "okay, but a long way away", and George explained the origin of the word "grotty" – "It means grotesque".

Prior to the screening, The Beatles were presented on the stage to wild applause, and when it was revealed that Ringo would be twenty-four the following day, the audience began spontaneously to sing "Happy Birthday Dear Ringo". With tickets priced from £1 to 15 guineas, the premiere raised £7,000 [£80,000 today] for the Variety Club of Great Britain's heart fund.

The *Daily Mirror* loved *A Hard Day's Night*. "This film wins all the way", Dick Richards announced in his review. "It's THAT film with THOSE boys – at last!" Shooting had begun, under the working title *Beatlemania*, in March and had been concluded in April, but fans had been kept waiting until now while the footage was edited, and while The Beatles visited the farthest corners of the globe on their world tour.

"We want to present their almost Goon-like quality", producer Walter Shenson had stated from the outset. "We are taking a lot of care about this because we don't want any junk, any sort of

cheap quickie. I look upon this film as having worldwide popularity. The beat these kids dig is international."

In his *Mirror* review Richards continued: "What could have been simply a money-making gimmick turns out as nimble entertainment in its own right." "It's off-beat – and on the beat. It's a winner." The film's simplicity was one of its highlights, he added. "A somewhat exaggerated idea of what might well happen in 36 hours in the wacky lives of these remarkable lads. John, Paul, George and Ringo come through as distinct characters. Cheeky, irreverent, funny, irresistible. All handle their scenes with unexpected confidence. Much credit must go to Richard Lester. He has directed with vital speed and inventiveness."

The film won further praise for its soundtrack. "There is no contrived, tedious background music", wrote Patrick Doncaster. "Action is not bolstered by any frantic score. Just songs . . . Songs by Lennon and McCartney. Exciting songs. Hit songs. There is not one that would not stand on its own in the charts. Yet John and Paul wrote so many songs for the film that they all could not be included in the finished product. The rest are on an LP record bearing the film title." ■

This page and facing page: Relaxing on 31 March between takes of *A Hard Day's Night* at the Scala Theatre, off Tottenham Court Road, London. This was the finale in which The Beatles finally got to record a TV appearance for their beleaguered director, played by Victor Spinetti. Plans to film them playing in front of 1,200 extras were thwarted when the Film Artistes Association called a strike to protest about unpaid

labour. While the union politics held up production, the hundreds of extras grew restless outside the theatre, some scaling walls and others climbing onto the roof trying to get in. A compromise was only reached when the number of fans was reduced to just 350, each of whom were paid for their day's work with £3 15 shillings in cash, a cheese lunch, a pork pie and a banana.

"Merseybeat Marxes!"

"HOW DO THE boys do it?", continued Patrick Doncaster in his *Mirror* review. "They produced the new songs for the film in spare moments between weeks of hard day's nights. Weeks that included a visit to Paris and America. Weeks that made spare time as difficult to find as diamonds in the Thames. Lennon and McCartney are a sort of sausage machine that churns out crochets and quavers – with lashings of extra seasoning and sauce."

Other reviews were just as ecstatic. "Yeah, yeah, yeah, yeah, yeah, yeah" wrote Robert Bickford in the *Daily Mail*. "It's got to be six times for the six bouncing new songs in this film. The title song is a wow. It starts with a curious plangent chord, then it hammers along at a rate that makes even the classic 'She Loves You' sound like a throw-out from the vicarage glee concert. Only one thing spoils it – the odd, tinkling fade-out. It should have finished with a bang."

> ## "Sausage machine . . . with lashings of extra seasoning and sauce."

Beneath the headline "Merseybeat Marxes!", the *Daily Mail*'s Cecil Wilson wrote, "The Marx Brothers exploded back on to the screen last night. Except that this time they were four adenoidal young anarchists from Liverpool who call themselves The Beatles. Up to now we have known Paul, John, Ringo and George as a singing group with a natural zaniness that turned every interview into a comic act. In their first film, shown last night to Princess Margaret, they emerge as a comedy act who also happen to play and sing."

The *Daily Telegraph*, while more reserved, was just as positive. "With their first feature film The Beatles have repeated their success of night club, theatre and television", wrote Patrick Gibbs. "They are much helped by the humour of Alun Owen's script, tactful handling by the director, Richard Lester, and the support of half a dozen useful players."

Of The Beatles themselves, Gibbs concluded: "Actors they may not be, but personalities they certainly remain, engagingly provocative and wonderfully photogenic." ∎

"It's off-beat – and on the beat. It's a winner."

DICK RICHARDS, *DAILY MIRROR*

Above: The Beatles flying into Speke Airport on 10 July to attend the Northern premiere of *A Hard Day's Night*. A large crowd of fans – some estimates suggested more than 200,000 – assembled outside a civic reception held at Liverpool Town Hall.

Left: Pattie Boyd and three *A Hard Day's Night* extras – from left to right, Tina Williams, Pru Bury and Susan Whitman – groom their idols at Twickenham Film Studios. "Their hair is on their heads, not on their chests", suggested the *Sunday Telegraph*.

Right, top: John blows a raspberry on a Liverpool Police Band euphonium at the civic reception.

Right: Filming the finale to *A Hard Day's Night* at the Scala Theatre, Scala Street, London, on 31 March.

Flying Ballet

THE NIGHT OF A HUNDRED STARS was an annual fund-raiser presented by the Actors' Charitable Trust. The all-night revue at the London Palladium began at midnight on 23 July, and John donated one of his drawings, a female caricature, for use as the front cover to the souvenir programme.

The show was hosted by Sir Laurence Olivier and boasted a bill featuring "stars of stage, screen and disc", including Judy Garland, Frankie Vaughan, Max Bygraves, Harry Secombe, Jane Asher and Zsa Zsa Gabor, plus Harry H. Corbett and Wilfred Brambell from *Steptoe & Son*. Standard repertoires were dispensed with as each star delivered an act as different from their usual performance as possible.

Representing "pop music", The Beatles couldn't help but play their hits, but in an additional sketch in the first half of the show, they literally rose to the challenge by performing a "Flying Ballet", in which they sang the *Peter Pan* song, "I'm Flying", while being hoisted into the air in four harnesses. The event raised a total of £11,000 [£124,500] for the Combined Theatrical Charities Appeals Council. ■

Above left: Running through "I'm Flying" with sketch director Joseph Kirby.

Insets: Larking about behind the scenes at the Palladium; Zsa Zsa Gabor talking to a busy Paul.

Left and below: Mingling with Cilla Black and the show's producers Lance Hamilton and Charles Russell on 23 July prior to the performance.

Facing page: The Beatles hoisted up on harnesses on 14 July, rehearsing their "Flying Ballet" sketch for *The Night of A Hundred Stars* midnight revue.

Five Nights at the Seaside

IN BETWEEN their world tour in June and their second visit to the United States in August, The Beatles played a series of five summer Sunday shows at British seaside resorts.

Jimmy Nicol, momentarily elevated to band leader status with The Shubdubs, supported them in Brighton on 12 July, while in Bournemouth on 2 August that honour went to The Kinks.

On 16 August, on the second of two visits to Blackpool (they had visited in July to appear on ITV's *Blackpool Night Out*), the *Mirror* photographed The Beatles in the shadow of the town's famous Blackpool Tower. One of the support acts that night was The High Numbers, a young R&B group featuring Pete Townshend, Roger Daltrey, John Entwistle and Keith Moon.

Beatlemania was alive and well in Scarborough, Yorkshire, the week before. The Beatles flew up to RAF Leconfield, twenty-five miles from the town, and drove to the Futurist Theatre in a limousine.

Approaching the venue, 2,000 fans engulfed the car, trapping it near the side entrance so that only John could open his door. One by one, The Beatles had to jump over the bonnet to reach the safety of the theatre.

The vagaries of driving for The Beatles was revealed in *The People* in August by their ex-chauffeur Bill Corbett: "When I took the job nine months ago I found I had to start learning an entirely new technique of driving. The art of moving off through a dense mob of half-crazed Beatles fans is something no driving school teaches."

"The biggest menace", he continued, "is not the fans thronging round the front of the car. A gentle nudge with the bumper, accompanied by a blast on the hooter, usually gets them out of the way. It is the girls clinging on to the door handles who worry me. If I drive away too slowly they will try to climb into the car or on to the roof. If I put my foot down and speed away they will still cling on desperately and be dragged dangerously along the road." ■

Left, top: John, Paul and Ringo lounge about on a hotel sofa in Blackpool, while Derek Taylor, Neil Aspinall and Brian Epstein talk logistics in the background. The Beatles were in town on 19 July to appear on ABC TV's *Blackpool Night Out* **with Mike and Bernie Winters.**

Left: The Beatles with support singer Cherry Rowland.

Below: The group's limousine gets trapped near the stage door of the Futurist Theatre, Scarborough, on 9 August after inching through the crowd. Some fans "seem to have no fear of injury or even death in the cause of Beatle-worship", observed their former chauffeur, Bill Corbett. "But I soon learned how to deal with them."

Below: The calm before the storm. The Beatles on a big night out in Blackpool where they staged their last British show of the summer at the town's Opera House on 16 August, before flying out to San Francisco the following day for a month-long tour of the US.

The First American Tour

ON 19 AUGUST, The Beatles flew across the Atlantic for what was billed as their First American Tour, a twenty-four-city, coast-to-coast trek which took in thirty-two shows in thirty-four days.

It had taken six months to organise — "as much planning as the invasion of Normandy" — and involved 22,500 miles of travelling, and over sixty hours' flying time. The tour was as ambitious as it was exhausting: in contrast to Britain's 3,000- and 4,000-seat venues, they now played to crowds ranging from 13,000 to 30,000. "Each one of us lost half a stone in sweat", remembered their roadie Mal Evans.

In the Deep South, The Beatles refused to play a concert at Jacksonville's Gator Bowl, Florida, until they'd been assured that black members of the audience would not be seated at the back of the stadium. "We never play to segregated audiences and we're not going to start now", insisted John. "I'd rather lose our appearance money."

At the Hollywood Bowl, the towels used to mop their Beatle brows were cut into tiny pieces and sold to fans for several dollars apiece. In New York local cowboys marketed cans of "Beatle Breath", while others made genuine offers to hoteliers for the group's dirty bathwater.

The epicentre of the madness proved to be Kansas City. Here, too, the linen was stripped from their hotel beds and sold, unwashed, to entrepreneurs who charged fans $10 for a three-inch square. And it was here that Charles O. Finley, millionaire manager of the local baseball team, saw to it that The Beatles worked on one of their few days off.

Kansas had been left off the tour itinerary, so Finley offered $50,000 [£18,000], more than the going rate, to include it. Realising that his boys were already seriously overworked, Brian Epstein refused. The offer was increased, and increased again until, at $150,000 [£54,000 then, £611,000 today], a deal was struck. At a rate of £1,785 per minute, The Beatles had broken another record: the largest fee ever paid for a single concert performance in America.

Despite that, the show didn't sell out and Finley lost thousands. But he didn't care; he'd bought The Beatles. But they had the last laugh. He'd asked them to play two extra songs. They gave him one: "Kansas City"/"Hey, Hey Hey". ∎

Left: On what should have been their day off on 17 September, The Beatles announce a hastily arranged show at the Kansas City Municipal Stadium in Missouri in front of 20,280 fans. The stadium seated 41,000.

Below: Making a splash in Los Angeles on 24 August during a rest day at the end of the first week of their US tour, The Beatles relax by the pool at the Bel Air mansion owned by British actor Reginald Owens.

Top: Mal Evans keeps guard from the right at the Forest Hills Tennis Stadium in New York on 28 August.

Above: Back to the camera, George enjoys a game of Monopoly with singer-songwriter Jackie de Shannon, one of the tour's support acts, at the Lafayette Motor Inn, Atlantic City, on 30 August.

Left: The Beatles play before the Stars and Stripes on the second night of their US tour, at the Convention Center, Las Vegas, Nevada.

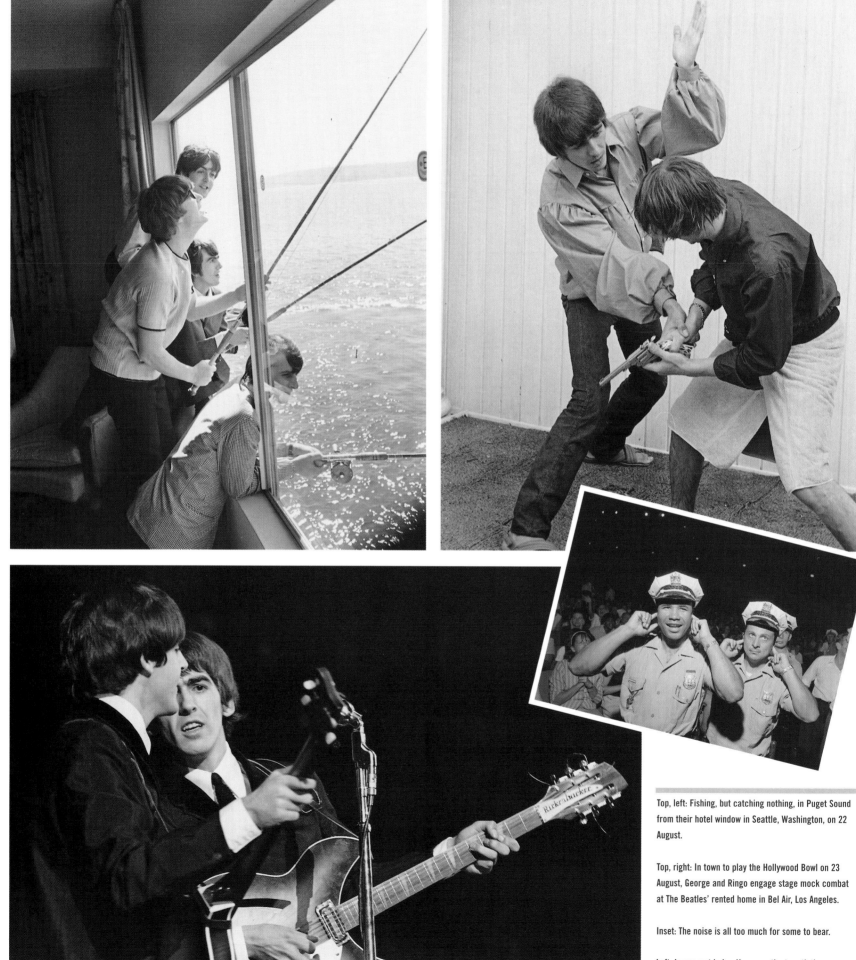

Top, left: Fishing, but catching nothing, in Puget Sound from their hotel window in Seattle, Washington, on 22 August.

Top, right: In town to play the Hollywood Bowl on 23 August, George and Ringo engage stage mock combat at The Beatles' rented home in Bel Air, Los Angeles.

Inset: The noise is all too much for some to bear.

Left: In concert in Las Vegas on the twentieth.

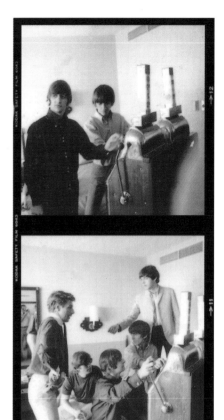

Left : At the poolside in Bel Air, where The Beatles spent two days in retreat on 24 and 25 August.

Below and right: Unable to visit the casino at the Sahara Hotel, Las Vegas, on 20 August, due to a Beatlemania alert on the ground floor, the casino is brought to them. Derek Taylor digs deep for some spare change.

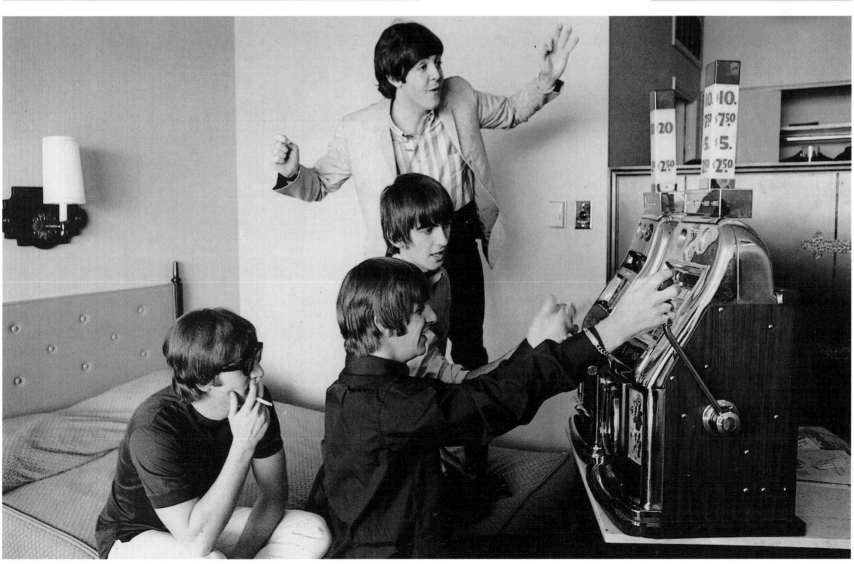

Top: With Dean Martin's daughter, Claudia, at a garden party in Los Angeles on the twenty-fourth.

Above: Ringo in his New York hotel room on the twenty-eighth with one of his most ardent fans.

Right: Soaking up the sun on the roof of the Sahara Hotel in Vegas.

Bottom, left: John and Paul escaping frenzied reporters at the Forest Hills Tennis Stadium, New York.

Bottom, right: Leaving New York City's John F. Kennedy Airport on 21 September, at the end of the tour.

Beat Time

RINGO WAS THE first Beatle to resurface after arriving back from their US tour. On 27 September, as the rest of the group enjoyed a weekend off, he occupied the principal position on a panel of judges at the final of the National Beat Group Competition, sponsored by Oxfam. The show, featuring eleven unknown bands, took place at London's Prince of Wales Theatre, and was broadcast live on BBC 2 as *It's Beat Time*.

The show was hosted by DJ David Jacobs, and included among the judges Brian Epstein, Cilla Black, Billy Hatton from The Fourmost, Betty Hale of *Fabulous* magazine, Pye Records' Alan Freeman and fifteen-year-old Linda Lewis from Oxford, who was chosen from eleven teenage panellists who'd served on earlier heats.

Despite the prestige of the occasion, and the fact that several of the contestants issued records, little again was ever heard of The Southerns, The Connoisseurs, The Starfires, The Apaches, Formula Five, The Down-Beats, The Vibros, The Countdowns, Roy Stuart & the Cyclones, Danny Clarke & the Jaguars or The Crusaders. ■

On the Wane?

THE BEATLES BEGAN their Autumn Tour of the UK's provinces – fifty-four shows on twenty-seven dates – to persistent rumours that they'd had their day. The papers all-too-gleefully reported on "rows of empty seats" at the first show at the Gaumont Cinema in Bradford on 9 October, and that the only shouts from fans in the street prior to the show had been for The Rolling Stones.

Worse still, no less a commentator than The Beatles' former ally the Duke of Edinburgh was reported to have said, "The Beatles are on the wane". But after the remark was printed in the papers, Prince Philip took the unprecedented step of ordering a telegram to be sent to Brian Epstein, denying responsibility. "Disregard press reports quoting the Duke of Edinburgh as saying Beatles on the wane. Should read: 'I think Beatles are *away* at the moment'. Mistake probably due to a misprint. Prince Philip sends his best wishes for continued success." The telegram made the front page of the *Daily Mirror*, and brought a smile to Brian Epstein's face. "Maybe we'll frame it", he said.

Speaking on a visit to London, Chuck Berry was cynical. "Beatle-type music is falling off", he said, adding the ominous warning, "Even The Beatles will have to change their delivery – or die."

In November, a *Sunday Mirror* feature predicted that the coming year would bring with it a new sound. Decca A&R man Dick Rowe, who'd famously turned the group down in favour of Brian Poole & the Tremelos, was one of the quoted pundits. "The Beatles and the Rolling Stones still survive", he said, "in spite of rumours that their popularity is on the wane, but only because they are getting away from the deafening big beat sound. The trend is likely to be toward quieter and more melodic music."

An *Evening News* columnist thought otherwise: "The change, I believe", he wrote, "is to Country and Western vogue." When a hint of the development of The Beatles did come, it was by accident. "The first bit you hear on 'I Feel Fine' is feedback", John told Virginia Ironside in the *Daily Mail* on 27 November. "It was all a mistake. I was standing between Paul's amplifier and mine, and that was the result . . . but when we heard it we liked it so we left it in. Sounds a bit like an electric razor, doesn't it?" ∎

Above: Backstage at Bradford's Gaumont Cinema on the first night (9 October) of The Beatles only UK tour of the year, with Motown star Mary Wells whom they first heard about while in the States. As sold-out notices (below) were placed in front of theatre entrances, Brian Epstein put the empty seats at Bradford down to "a muddle over reservations".

Below: Caught on camera at the Kilburn State Ballrooms in London on 23 October – John looking away, Paul and Ringo looking happy, and George looking bad-tempered.

Facing page: George, Ringo, John, Paul, a wardrobe and a coat-stand in the dressing room of the De Monfort Hall, Leicester, on 10 October. "Screaming teenage girls gave The Beatles a wild welcome", reported the *Daily Mirror*, but the reception was still considered "mild" compared with their show at the same venue the previous December.

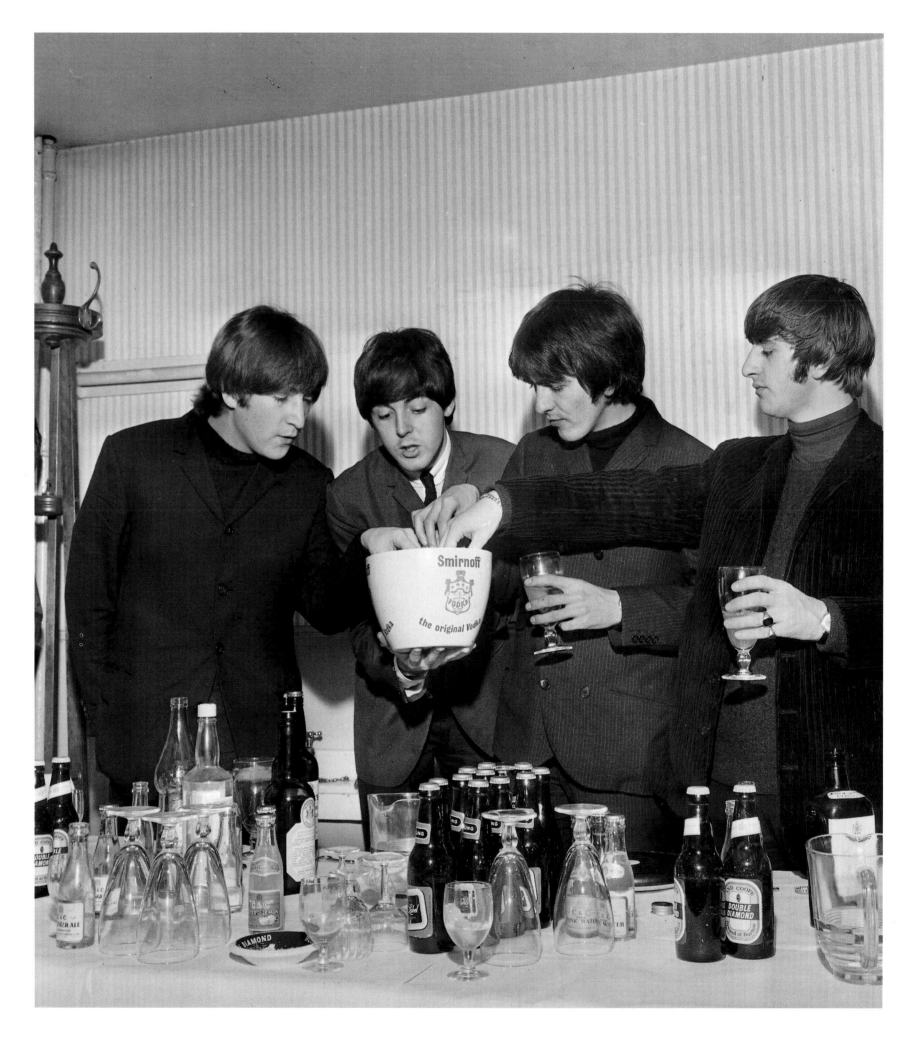

"Yeah, Yeah Yeah, Vote for Labour!"

THERE WAS NO sign of a decline in The Beatles' pulling power on 21 October when their tour reached Glasgow, where a mob of 3,000 frantic fans arrived for a concert at the Odeon Cinema. In a clumsy attempt at crowd control, 200 policemen, some of them mounted, jostled and pushed the teenagers away from the venue. Angered by the heavy-handedness, the fans retaliated by overturning two cars. Firemen rushed to the scene to douse the spilled petrol from the streets before disaster struck. "This is the first time we've met any violence of this kind in this country", said a Beatles spokesman. "But Glasgow is always a hot city."

The 1964 General Election took place in the middle of the tour, but The Beatles didn't vote. The *Daily Mail*, witnessing the end of thirteen years of Conservative rule, painted a picture of The Beatles as youthful sceptics. "We don't care a lot about politics", Paul was quoted, speaking from the group's hotel in Wigan, "so we never bothered to fix a postal vote." To which John added: "We've been away from Liverpool so long that we have forgotten what constituency we are in. It's a lot of rubbish, anyway."

"It's a lot of rubbish, anyway."

Backing Harold Wilson's winning Labour Party, the *Daily Mirror* ran with a different story: "We didn't get our voting papers in time", explained a "disappointed" Paul, just before going on stage in Stockton-on-Tees a day later. "We wanted to have postal votes, but our forms were sent off too late. That means we can't vote today, unless we go back to our own constituencies in Liverpool."

Soliciting The Beatles' political support was "Screaming" Lord Sutch, who stood against Harold Wilson in the Liverpool constituency of Huyton. "I stand for votes at eighteen", he stated in his manifesto, "no victimisation because of long hair, a knighthood for The Beatles and legalising (pirate) radio stations."

Despite not taking part in the election, The Beatles wouldn't be drawn publicly on which party or candidate they favoured. No one admitted responsibility, either, for the loud-speaker van cruising the queues at Stockton blaring out the message, "Yeah, yeah, yeah! Vote for Labour!"

Above: Cooling down the quiet one on the steps of the Liverpool Empire, where The Beatles played their first hometown concert for nearly a year on 8 November. With Beatlemania under firm control, Chief Constable Joseph Smith told the group after the show, "I want to thank you for all you've done for the city. You're a great bunch of guys."

Left: Ligging in Leeds with Double Diamond and lashings of lager. The Beatles help themselves to the hospitality backstage at a press reception at the Odeon Cinema on 22 October.

Right: Picking competition winners out of a hat in their Liverpool Empire dressing room.

"We're all the same."

THE BEATLES entered into a different kind of political debate when the Communist newspaper the *Daily Worker* interviewed John and Paul backstage at Bradford. Asked about their non-segregation stance on their American tour (leading to some dates falling through in the Southern states), Paul said it was because The Beatles thought that segregation was "daft".

"It's daft looking upon coloured people as some sort of freaks", he elaborated. "Before we went to the US someone told us they might try to segregate the audiences. We stuck in the clause just in case. We had coloured people with us in America. There was no discrimination there. The audience loved them. I don't think the kids over there are half as bigoted as their parents. They are a new generation."

John explained further: "In America they

Segregation is "daft".

accept the Negro as an entertainer. On that there is no prejudice. We didn't see any prejudice on the five weeks of the tour. We had Frogman Henry with us. He was born in the Deep South. We asked him where he'd rather live, he said in the South. You see, he's an entertainer. But segregation. They put them behind wire or something. Why should they? They all pay the same money. We're all the same." Discussing the progeny of racists, John wasn't as optimistic as Paul. "They're born into it", he said. "And it will take a long time for them to grow out of it."

The Beatles felt strongly enough about racial discrimination to have considered financially supporting those campaigning against apartheid in South Africa. "I may be putting my foot in it", said Paul, "but it would be an idea to give them the proceeds from the premiere of our new film. We're starting shooting next February. But, then, it might be booked already."

Mary Wells' presence on the UK Autumn Tour didn't warrant a mention in the interview. There was no political capital to be made out of her role as star support act, and it was explained elsewhere that The Beatles had heard Mary in America, and that in the wake of her hit, "My Guy", she'd been elevated to the status of "favourite singer". ■

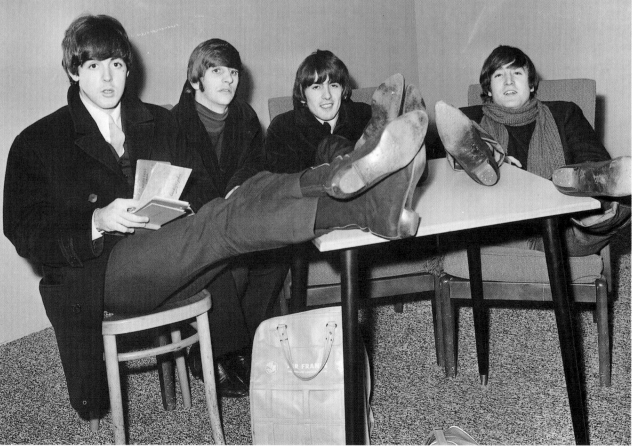

Still enormously popular

A MILD CONTROVERSY erupted in mid-October when The Beatles decided at the last minute to include Belfast on their Autumn Tour itinerary. As the papers discovered to their dismay, this meant that despite last year's triumph the group wouldn't be appearing at 1964's Royal Variety Performance on 2 November – leaving Cilla Black and The Bachelors (two of whom were married) to represent "the young idea".

"Were they invited?" asked the *Daily Mirror*, admitting "show business ethics dictate that no star can say publicly". Even if they had been, the reasoning followed, "it would be regarded as extreme bad taste to reject a Royal Show invitation". But The Beatles *had* turned the Queen down, and didn't mind admitting it either.

Ringo broke the unwritten showbiz rule by "exploding" when a reporter suggested that their

> ## "Nonsense, nonsense, nonsense."

absence from the Royal bill was down to their "fading popularity". "We *were* invited!" he fumed. John insisted that "there was never any intention to snub the Queen. Our tour took in Belfast as a late date, but the invitation came afterwards". To which Paul added, "Over 4,000 tickets had been sold for the Belfast show and we couldn't let the kids down". "Naturally", added George, "we are all disappointed."

As the tour approached its end, the American magazine *Newsweek* claimed that The Beatles were bored with one-night stands, world tours and, worse still, each other. They might give up touring and go into TV and films, Elvis-style. The *Daily Mirror* weighed in too, declaring "Beatlemania days are over. Not because the fans have lost interest – but because The Beatles are tired of whistle-stop tours."

"Nonsense, nonsense, nonsense", replied Brian Epstein. "There's no question of their giving up personal appearances. They will probably do *fewer* next year, but I think that nearness to their fans is important to The Beatles. They are still enormously popular with the record-buying public, and they have a duty towards them." George agreed with both arguments. "We love the fans", he said. "But tours like this are a drag." ■

Above: After a show at the King's Hall, Belfast, on 2 November, Ringo and Paul present plastic guns and guitars to local volunteers in a toys-for-Christmas campaign for the city's orphans.

Facing page, top: The Beatles photographed in London at the Kilburn State Ballrooms on 23 October. In nearby Highgate earlier in the month, similar pictures (perhaps ones in which George looked a little happier) were fixed to the ceilings and walls in an anaesthetic room in Whittington Hospital to help soothe children on their way to the operating theatre. "The pictures have worked wonders", a nurse told the *Daily Mirror*. "Most children, even young immigrants who perhaps cannot speak English, know and love The Beatles."

Facing page, bottom: A little leather sole on the table at the King's Hall, Belfast, as The Beatles relax backstage rather than play for the Queen at the Royal Variety Performance in London.

Right: In the week The Beatles' new single "I Feel Fine" enters the chart at No. 1, Ringo announces at a press conference at University Hospital that, six months after illness forced him off the first dates of The Beatles' world tour, he is finally having his tonsils taken out.

Below: Rehearsing on 22 December for *Another Beatles Christmas Show* at the Hammersmith Odeon. When asked about the costumes The Beatles had chosen for one of their comedy sketches, Ringo said, "We picked up on Eskimo gear because Eskimo-land seems to be about the only place we haven't visited this year. I think it's Greenland, or somewhere". In order that the routines

could be appreciated in spite of the noisy fan hysteria, producer Peter Yolland came up with the idea of projecting the group's dialogue onto stage scenery like sub-titles on a cinema screen.

Facing page, top: With the co-stars of their two comedy sketches, Freddie Garrity of Freddie & the Dreamers and DJ Jimmy Savile.

Facing page, bottom: The massed *Christmas Show* line-up including Elkie Brooks and members of The Yardbirds, Freddie & the Dreamers and Sounds Incorporated.

"Eskimo-land seems to be about the only place we haven't visited this year."

RINGO

CHAPTER THREE

1965

THEY HAD ONLY RECENTLY become famous. Now they were ubiquitous – cited in matters of world politics, anthropology, even horticulture. According to the Chinese newspaper *Ta Kung Pao*, they were "monsters who made an unpleasant noise to satisfy the Western World's need for crazy and rotten music"; which was a lighter approach than Indonesia's President Sukarno, who ordered his henchmen to "arrest anyone playing or singing Beatles songs". But the truth was out there. "You can walk down any street of the most primitive village in a country where no one speaks English", said Newcastle University's Professor Strang, "and hear the children chanting the words of the latest Beatles hit." And in America, where a gardening magazine conducted experiments with salad vegetables and various styles of music, it was discovered that even "radishes thrive on The Beatles".

> ## "They have been absorbed. They are ours."
>
> **VINCENT MULCHRONE, *DAILY MAIL***

Elsewhere, *Mary Poppins* pipped *A Hard Day's Night* at the Oscars, while *Help!* only managed a joint win of the "Golden Seagull" award at the Rio de Janeiro Film Festival. But The Beatles could still deny the Queen. In 1964 they'd turned down the invitation to the Royal Variety Performance, and now they declined to play at Windsor Castle's "Waterloo" society ball. "They don't do private functions", said a spokesman.

The snub didn't prevent Buckingham Palace honouring them as Ordinary Members of the Civil Division of the Most Excellent Order of the British Empire – MBEs – a move prompting outlandish outbursts from war veterans, politicians and newspaper columnists alike. Even The Beatles themselves didn't know quite what to say. "It's a good idea that younger people are getting the MBE now", fumbled Ringo. "Before, you got it when you were practically dead." And in a more materialistic frame of mind, George added: "I think I'll take my medal down the antique shop to see what it's made of." ■

Ringo and his new bride Maureen Cox hold a press conference on 12 February, at their seaside honeymoon home at 2 Prince's Crescent, Hove, East Sussex, a house owned by The Beatles' solicitor David Jacobs. The couple were married the previous day at Caxton Hall Register Office in London — at 8.00 a.m., to avoid the fans.

1965

■ The Beatles' publishing company, Northern Songs Ltd, was floated on the stock market in February. The 1,250,000 shares were so oversubscribed that City men predicted that prices "could top 9 shillings".

■ As The Beatles were awarded their MBEs in June, it was announced that they had directly contributed over £1 million [£10,800,000 today] to the Government in tax and export profits.

■ In June, the *Daily Mirror* reported that there were now 1,337 different recordings of the sixty Beatles'-penned songs. Of these, 365 were American, while Canada and Japan had 214 each.

■ A report in August revealed that £500,000 [£5,400,000] insurance policies had been taken out on the lives of John and Paul by Northern Songs

Ltd. The annual premium for both was £9,975 [£108,000].

■ By the summer, world sales of Beatles records had reached the equivalent of 115,000,000 singles.

■ Before their second US tour in August, The Beatles insured themselves at Lloyd's of London against non-appearance at concerts through sickness and injury for £1 million [£10,800,000] each.

■ At a New York auction in September, a concert programme signed by all four Beatles was valued at $250 (about £90), $90 more than a 100-year-old letter written by Brahms.

■ Northern Songs' first Annual General Meeting took place in Liverpool Street, London, in September, and was attended by Brian Epstein, fifty bowler-hatted shareholders, and one seventeen-year-old Beatles fan. Profits of £620,000 [£6,700,000] were recorded, "£100,000 up on expectations".

■ By the autumn, all four Beatles owned Minis. John and Ringo also had a Rolls-Royce each, while Paul and George had Aston Martins. John also owned a GT Ferrari and Volkswagen, and Ringo an Italian Facel Vega sports car.

■ When polling organisation Mass Observation Ltd asked 2,000 members of the public to identify people in the news, 96 per cent correctly named The Beatles. Ex-prime minister Sir Alec Douglas-Home only polled 83 per cent, and Great Train Robber Ronald Biggs 68 per cent.

A Cast of Minions

THE BEATLES' second film began production in February. Shot in colour, it would be "a mad, zany, wild comedy thriller", pledged producer Walter Shenson. "Definitely not like the first film."

The success of *A Hard Day's Night* ensured a twofold increase in the budget – £400,000 [£4,300,000] – and a script which called for exotic locations, special effects and a cast of minions: Asian thugs, the local constabulary, a real-life army division, famous British character actors like Patrick Cargill, Alfie Bass, Roy Kinnear and Warren Mitchell, and the twenty-six-year-old Eleanor Bron, "the outrageously funny mimic" who had recently made her name on the BBC's satirical show *Not So Much A Programme More A Way Of Life*.

Production began on 23 February with great expectations – "I've no doubt they can establish themselves as great screen personalities", Shenson said of John, Paul, George and Ringo – but without much of a plan. "We just throw the script up in the air", admitted director Richard Lester, "and shoot the first pages that float down."

Neither did the film have a firm title. It began life as *Beatles Two*, before the group suggested the naughtier *High-Heeled Knickers*. On 17 March, a "hard day's night"-style Ringo-ism, *Eight Arms To Hold You*, was officially announced to the press; until 15 April when, as production was nearing completion, Richard Lester finally came up with *Help!*.

Back in Britain after filming in the Bahamas and the Austrian alps, The Beatles spent three chilly days in early May, on Knighton Down, in Larkhill, Wiltshire. Just half-a-mile from Britain's prehistoric Stonehenge, this tiny windswept dot on Salisbury Plain was also a real-life military playground for the British Army.

As The Beatles mimed a take of George's "I Need You", eighty members of 3 Division – including infantry, machine-gunners, horse artillery and even Centurion tanks – manoeuvred onto the set to defend the group against the film's baddies, a marauding cult of Hindu extremists, intent on retrieving a sacrificial ring which had somehow become attached to one of Ringo's fingers.

Help! received its premiere on 29 July, at the London Pavilion, Piccadilly Circus, once again in the presence of Princess Margaret and Lord Snowdon, Anthony Armstrong-Jones. As with *A Hard Day's Night*, the Variety Club of Great Britain benefitted from the event, this time by £6,000 [£65,000]. Almost 12,000 people packed into Piccadilly Circus to glimpse the film's stars and attending royalty, prompting Westminster City Council to board up the famous statue of Eros to protect it from the crowd. ∎

Top and left: Ringo and John on the set of *Help!* on 14 April. Just two "ordinary lads" outside their communal Beatle pad in Ailsa Avenue, Twickenham.

Above: Ringo, Raja and Eleanor Bron at Twickenham on 28 May. Raja is the "famous Bengal man-eater" in *Help!*

Inset: What Donald Zec described as "The Magnificent Seven", marking the production launch of *Help!*: Brian Epstein (standing, far left), Richard Lester (centre), Walter Shenson (right) and The Beatles.

Half Marx

ADMITTING THAT the new film was little more than a technicolour comic strip, Richard Lester said prior to the screening: "You'll find nothing new about *Help!* There's not one bit of insight into a social phenomenon of our times."

But Princess Margaret approached it as a fan, reminding Ringo of his uncertainty over *A Hard Day's Night*. "You were a trifle pessimistic about that one", she said. "I enjoyed it very much and I have been looking forward to this one. I've come with an open mind." To which Paul added, "Well, it's not as bad as Donald Zec says it is!"

Zec's review in the *Daily Mirror* had been damning; only the *Daily Express* was wholly positive: "Marvellous!" it said. "Any lucky fools might have made a good first film. But to make a good second film – that's the test The Beatles triumphantly, effortlessly, nonchalantly, and above all cheerfully, survive with *Help!* Mr Lester's

> ## "The camera practically throttled itself with its own contortions."

direction is a joy to watch. He does outrageously corny things with the cameras and colours. But, of course, The Beatles are the film, and this at least is no flash in the pan. These boys are the closest thing to the Marx Brothers since the Marx Brothers."

The *Sketch* bridged the gap with Robert Ottaway's guarded comment that "no amount of deft invisible mending can disguise the fact that, basically, the film is made from a dated pattern . . . the mechanics of the plot begin to creak after the first half-hour".

Then came the outspoken Mr Z: "I didn't roll in the aisle, my sides remained unsplit", he wrote, "so my verdict on the new Beatles film must be Half Marx."

The exotic locations and the lack of a credible plot also came in for a grilling from Zec. The former "gave Richard Lester some great opportunities for some visual gags, and he milked them until the camera practically throttled itself with its own contortions"; while the latter meant that the film "leaned heavily on the likable vacant grin of John Lennon, the smooth charm of Paul, the long-haired good looks of George and the darkly villainous looks of the Long-Nosed One. Not enough to carry a movie in my view". ■

Above and left: On the set of *Help!*, shooting the scenes in which they attempt an "acoustical experiment in sound" in a natural amphitheatre at Knighton Down, Salisbury Plain. In the background is the kind of security only The Beatles could demand: the British Army's 3 Division, complete with infantry, gunners and Centurion tanks.

Right: Ringo feels the chill factor.

Above: The Beatles with Eleanor Bron at London Airport on 22 February about to fly out to Nassau in the Bahamas to begin shooting *Help!*

Left and facing page: Scenes from the film shoot at the London suburb of Strand-on-the-Green, Chiswick, on 24 April. Fleeing from Clang at one end and the police at the other, The Beatles run into a crowd of thugs dressed as Scottish bagpipers. "Gerroff!" says Ringo, as Paul gives a constable a slap. "Whose side are you on? We want protection."

Top: On 9 May the *Help!* location shoot moved to a side street off London's Marylebone Road where, "seeking enlightenment", The Beatles head for an Indian restaurant. Alfie Bass is the doorman from Stepney, East London.

Above and right: Fleeing from Clang, the chief baddie in the film, The Beatles make a quick getaway from a pub by crashing through the window rather than walking out the door. This scene was shot on 24 April at the City Barge, Strand-on-the-Green.

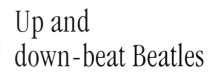

Up and down-beat Beatles

THE FINANCIAL implications of being The Beatles' drummer and their ex-drummers were revealed in several *Daily Mirror* stories at the end of April. "A Beatle's mum has moved from her £1 10s-a-week dockland home into an £8,000 bungalow", the paper reported on the twenty-fourth. "I didn't want to move — I lived in that little house for twenty years", said Mrs Elsie Starkey, the mother of Ringo. "But Richie — that's what I call him — pleaded with me to move. He didn't want to be the odd-Beatle-out. The other boys have bought luxury homes for their parents."

At the other end of the scale were ex-Beatles Pete Best and Jimmy Nicol. On 28 April the *Mirror* told how Pete too might have become a millionaire, but had instead found himself unemployed now that the beat-boom was in decline. His own group, which didn't warrant a name-check, had packed it in, he said, "rather than play for buttons". Back in 1962, he and The Beatles had been earning £45 [£540] per night,

> ## "The worst thing that ever happened to me."

but his most recent show had netted a measly £7 and 10 shillings. "I was with The Beatles two-and-a-half years", he said. "I try to forget. Though in moments of depression, I think on where I might have been . . . and where I am now."

Just one day later, temporary Beatle Jimmy Nicol was declared bankrupt at a court in London, with debts of £4,066 [£44,000] and just £50 [£550] to his name. "Standing in for Ringo was the worst thing that ever happened to me", he admitted. Sporting a distinctive Beatle-style haircut, he added: "Up until then I was feeling quite happy turning over £30 to £40 a week. I didn't realise that it would change my whole life. I had a half-a-million pounds worth of publicity and immediately I was offered three weeks at Blackpool standing in for Dave Clark at £350 a week. Everyone in showbusiness said I couldn't miss. I was the hottest name there was. But after the headlines died, I began dying too. No one wanted to know me any more. I borrowed from everyone and anyone." Ringo's response offered little solace: "I didn't think he could fail. No one did."

Top: Ringo and Cilla Black try out a new dance, The Skip, on 25 January, at a party in "'Appy 'Ampstead" thrown by *Melody Maker* journalist Bob Dawburn.

Top, right and below: Pete Best at home in Liverpool, and Jimmy Nicol round his mum's house in Battersea.

Above: John in George Martin's car in the EMI Studios' car park on 15 January, having passed his driving test.

Right: The Beatles with two American fans, Mary and Virginia Pezzullo. The two had flown over from New York City just to see *Another Beatles Christmas Show* and were rewarded with a backstage meet-and-greet.

Stupidity and Hysteria!

WIDESPREAD INCREDULITY and outrage broke out on 12 June, when it was announced in the Queen's Birthday Honours List that The Beatles had been awarded MBEs.

The recommendation had been made on the advice of Prime Minister Harold Wilson, which prompted critic Bernard Levin to write in the *Daily Mail*: "What humiliates us all about Mr. Wilson's action is precisely that it has set the State's most formal stamp of approval on the mindless and ephemeral rubbish which the Beatles' music is." In the *Daily Mirror*, meanwhile, a merely mildly piqued Donald Zec admitted that The Beatles were "a nice bunch of chaps" but concluded giving them MBEs was "hilarious, bordering on the absurd".

Letters from the public poured into Buckingham Palace by the hundred condemning the awards, many of them containing returned medals. One, from Squadron-Leader Paul Pearson, claimed that the honour had now become "debased and cheapened"; while another contained a vituperative rant from the French Canadian MP Hector Dupuis: "I certainly don't want to be associated with those long-haired, vulgar nincompoops. Neither do I wish to be a member of an Order which recognises stupidity and hysteria."

The *Mail*'s editorial was equivocal. "Strum the electric guitar", it began, "and beat the bongos, yeah, yeah, yeah. St James's Palace is switched on at last." It then went on, none too seriously, to decry the fact that other pop stars had been overlooked. "What about Sandie Shaw, who might have gone to the investiture in her bare feet? What about The Dave Clark Five, The Bachelors, The Animals? What honour should have been conferred on The Rolling Stones? (There is no need to answer that one.)"

Left, top and bottom: At Brian Epstein's Saville Theatre in London on 26 October, after receiving their insignia from the Queen at Buckingham Palace. "If they'd been made dukes I doubt whether they'd be surprised", wrote the *Evening Standard*.

Below and right: Honoured but underwhelmed. On 12 June while at Twickenham Film Studios to view a rough cut of *Help!*, The Beatles gave a press conference about their MBE awards, which had been announced that morning.

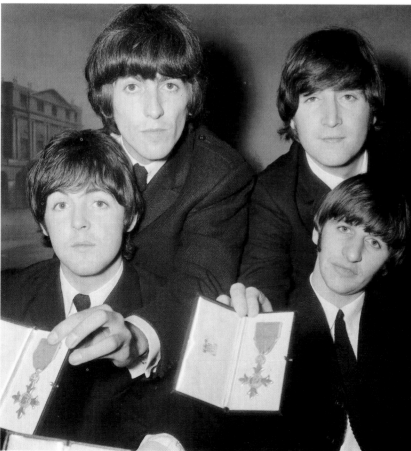

"Jane and I have not been Albufeira, as the

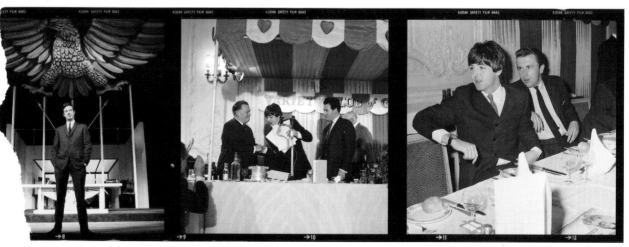

Above, left and right: Paul and Jane Asher arriving back from a holiday in Albufeira, Portugal, on 11 June – a day early in order to be in the country as The Beatles MBE awards are announced the following day.

Right, from left to right: Brian Epstein on 11 June at the Saville Theatre on London's Shaftesbury Avenue, the lease of which he'd taken over in April; Paul is greeted by Sir Billy Butlin at the Savoy Hotel on 13 July – host Keith Fordyce is also visible; and Paul and David Frost at the Variety Club lunch on 13 July at which he accepted five Ivor Novello songwriting awards on behalf of The Beatles.

married in rumours said."

PAUL McCARTNEY

Right: The Beatles on 4 July, arriving back at London Airport from Spain, the last stop-off point on a two-week tour of Europe.

Below: "It's over there!" An airport official points the way to the plane as The Beatles leave London on 13 August for a ten-date tour of the States. While in Beverly Hills, they meet Elvis.

Taking us for Granted?

BLACKPOOL NIGHT OUT, filmed on 1 August at the town's ABC Theatre, had been planned as a summer highlight for The Beatles. Their TV appearances had been scant of late and this was their only UK slot to promote *Help!*

It was also the first time a Beatle performed solo: Paul with his acoustic rendition of "Yesterday". But in the eyes of the *Mirror*'s critics, the programme fell short of another anticipated TV triumph. The show was broadcast live, and required an afternoon's rehearsal with its comedian hosts Mike and Bernie Winters, even if the group eventually failed to take part in a comedy sketch which had been specially written for them. Aside from briefly joining in with a line of dancing chorus girls, The Beatles stuck to what they did best – music.

"It was a pity they didn't do something a little different", rued Ken Irwin in the *Mirror*'s Northern edition the following day, before dishing out the back-handed praise: "The boys may sing out of key and may play slightly out of tune but, by golly, they have an excitement no other group can match."

Writing in the London edition, Clifford Davis decided that even the thrills of The Beatles playing poorly was a let down. The show "doubtless came up with everything their fans expected", he said. "For my money, however, I missed the pace and excitement of their previous TV appearances." Worse was to come: "Much of the fun was missing, too. And I think John Lennon could have been rather more gracious to the theatre audience in his remarks at the close. I don't think any performer can afford to take any audience for granted . . . I think they ought to work a little harder."

Perhaps The Beatles were fed up. Brian Epstein had long been unhappy with their guest appearances, as he realised that TV's sound reproduction could never match that of a "gramophone recording studio". This offended his sense of excellence; just days later it was announced that there would be no Beatles' Christmas show this year, and that plans to pipe a performance to selected cinemas via closed-circuit TV had also been shelved.

"The Christmas show is something we have done for two years", Brian explained. "However, The Beatles will never repeat the same formula, and it is certainly not my way of doing things.

"At present we have no plans. There may be an odd television engagement or appearance, but that's all." ■

Top, left: Opportunity knocks for Paul McCartney of Liverpool as he makes his debut solo appearance singing "Yesterday".

Inset: Ringo with Bernie Winters, one of the show's hosts.

Left, top right, facing page and overleaf: The novelty begins to wear off on *Blackpool Night Out* on 1 August, as The Beatles rehearse a performance that's "out of key" and "slightly out of tune". John Lennon performing live on keyboards is a rare sight.

"An excitement no other group can match."

DAILY MIRROR

The Music Of Lennon & McCartney

THAT "ODD TELEVISION ENGAGEMENT" became *The Music Of Lennon & McCartney*, a fifty-five-minute TV spectacular advertising John and Paul's songwriting talents.

George and Ringo joined in for performances of The Beatles' new single, "Day Tripper"/"We Can Work It Out" – and on the latter John swapped his guitar for the Granada studio harmonium, as played by Ena Sharples in *Coronation Street*.

The bulk of the show featured a gaggle of guest artists singing Beatles' songs, each introduced by John and Paul; among them Cilla Black ("It's For You"), Lulu ("I Saw Him Standing There"), Esther Philips ("And I Love Him"), Peter & Gordon ("A World Without Love"), and Marianne Faithfull ("Yesterday"). Peter Sellers recited "A Hard Day's Night" in the style of Sir Laurence Olivier's *Richard III*.

The programme was made in November by producer Johnny Hamp, and became "the biggest musical show we've ever put on". Hamp had

been the man behind The Beatles' TV debut on the regional *People And Places*, back in 1962 during the "Love Me Do" period.

"I first saw The Beatles in a club in Hamburg", he told the *Daily Mirror*. "They were very scruffy characters indeed – but they had a beat in their music which I liked. I put them on one of our shows. I got into trouble over it. Everyone said they were too rough, too untidy. But I liked them and put them on again and again."

That first TV appearance had earned the group £35 [£400]. In contrast, *The Music Of Lennon & McCartney* cost £20,000 [£215,000] to stage, half of which went to John and Paul. The show was a financial success before it hit the screens. "We'll get our money back", assured Hamp. "Already, we've had offers from all over the world to buy it." ∎

Left, top and strip, far left: John and Paul with Johnny Hamp, the producer who booked The Beatles for their TV debut back in 1962. The white circular cage in the picture is a model of the studio set.

Left, bottom: Sue Gerrard and June Speakland, two of the "bevy of showgirls" (strip below), who appear in the show, discuss their plans for the evening with Paul and John.

Above: Paul and John talk tactics as toy soldiers double as real-life Beatles on Johnny Hamp's scale model of *The Music Of Lennon & McCartney* stage set.

Left: Sitting on the sofa with a Beatle or two. Lulu, who sings "I Saw Him Standing There" in the show, is flanked by John and Paul.

CHAPTER FOUR

1966

BEATLEMANIA SUBSIDED into Beatlephobia. International opposition continued as South Africa banned their records; as did Israel, claiming that "their performance lacks artistic value and their appearance causes disorder". Beatle-style tresses were snipped from the heads of teenagers in Indonesia by scissor-wielding policemen. And now the hair-scare even made it to Australia. "We are saving a generation from itself", said a spokesman for the New South Wales authorities, giving "hair inspectors" the power to impose fines on factory workers wearing the Beatle-cut. The Beatles were booed and manhandled while on tour in the Philippines, after failing to meet President and Mrs Marcos in Manila. Worse still were the bonfires in Birmingham, Alabama, as American DJs took offence to John's "anti-Christian" remarks that "Jesus was alright but his disciples were thick and ordinary". As pyres of the group's records burned in a frenzy of fundamentalism, the *Daily Telegraph* warned of "the twilight of The Beatles". In Britain, the widening gap between John's old "today image" and the group's new tomorrow was highlighted when a schoolteacher discovered that their songs couldn't be translated into Latin. "In Roman times", he said, "women were subservient. They weren't free to decide on romance or to be persuaded. Beatles numbers are nearly all about love." But The Beatles had already moved on. "Neither side has any romance about it", the *Daily Mirror* said of the single "Paperback Writer"/"Rain". "These are the songs of '66, looking at life instead of at dreams and heart-pangs." The *Sunday Mirror* wasn't so keen. "They have, to put it bluntly, goofed", it claimed. "'Paperback Writer' would have gone into my junk box had it been by another group." John and Paul all but agreed, admitting that "it is not one of our best songs".

> **"Have you noticed how square The Beatles have become?"**
>
> *SUNDAY MIRROR*

Tax, Man

"IT'S MOSTLY A MATTER OF TAX", a NEMS spokesman admitted to the *Sunday Mirror* in June. The paper, like most others, had been wondering what the group was up to, and why their lengthy silence?

There had been no new record for the last six months, and no UK concert tour for the last seventeen. They hadn't been on TV much either; even their brief appearance at the annual *NME* Poll Winners' Concert in May wasn't televised due to age-old "contractual disagreements", which boiled down, once again, to Brian Epstein's dissatisfaction with the quality of TV's sound reproduction. "If they worked any more than they do", added the NEMS man, "it would be for nothing."

The dearth of news had left the papers wanting. Ringo's temporary sprouting of a beard in mid-January was greeted with unheard-of enthusiasm, but in reality the story was little more than a caption to a photograph. George had married Pattie Boyd in January, but the seven-minute ceremony at Esher Register Office had

been conducted in secret. (This left Paul the only single Beatle and he, the *Daily Mirror* reported, was "going steady" with actress Jane Asher.)

Paul had decided to buy a remote 183-acre dairy farm near the Mull of Kintyre in Scotland, but wouldn't be moving in until next November – so that was a non-story. There had been idle talk that he (and perhaps John) would be writing a symphony with Richard Rodney Bennett for the London Philharmonic Orchestra; but other than that, "our private lives are our own affair", said John.

What the group had actually been doing all this time was recording the LP *Revolver*. "We are experimenting all the time with our sound", Paul told the *Daily Mirror*'s Patrick Doncaster in June. "We cannot stay in the same rut. We have got to move forward. Our new LP is going to shock a lot of people." ■

Above left and inset: Paul and Jane Asher and George and Pattie with Cilla Black arrive at the Plaza Cinema, Haymarket, London, on 24 March for the Alfie premiere.

Left and facing page: After being manhandled in Manila by disgruntled Filipinos John was similarly accosted by fans as The Beatles arrived back at London Airport on 8 July (main picture) from their tour of the Far East.

Facing page, top, left: "I hate shaving. Now I'm on holiday I don't have to", said Ringo when reporters asked him why he'd grown a beard. The new face furniture was first noticed when Ringo and Maureen passed through London Airport on 12 January en route to Port of Spain in Trinidad, for a holiday with John and Cynthia. From Trinidad, John and Ringo sent a cabled message to the Daily Mirror and its readers.

1966

■ In April, the *News of the World* reported that in three years, John Lennon and Paul McCartney have written more than ninety songs that have been recorded in 2,921 versions and sold 200,000,000 copies, worth nearly £20,000,000 [£207,000,000 today].

■ The American LP *Yesterday And Today* was withdrawn in June at a cost of $80,000 [£29,000] because the "Butcher" cover was considered "too offensive". "In the centre is the severed head of a doll", wrote the *Daily Mirror*. "The Beatles are grinning."

■ By early July, the *Daily Sketch* reported that "Paperback Writer" had sold 500,000 copies in the UK, "less than half the advance orders they accrued in their heyday".

■ The Beatles' final tour visited the US in August. It lasted seventeen days, and earned them $1,000,000 [£360,000 then, £3,700,000 today].

■ In the wake of John's "more popular than Jesus" furore in August, shares in Northern Songs dropped by two shillings, losing Lennon and McCartney £140,000 [£1,450,000] overnight.

■ Some 8,000 protestors joined an anti-Beatles pro-Jesus demonstration in Memphis, Tennessee, when The Beatles played two shows there on 19 August.

■ In September a five-shilling pamphlet tracing The Beatles' genealogical history revealed that Ringo's family name, Starkey, dated back to 1260 and meant "dry and unyielding".

Top, centre: "Note George Harrison wearing a cap and small square glasses", advised the *Mirror* as The Beatles flew out to Munich on 23 June, for their first concerts in Germany since January 1963.

Strip, from top to bottom: Pattie Boyd returns to modelling on 21 April, for the first time since her marriage to George; Mr and Mrs H "unnoticed by the crowd" leave London's Garrick Theatre on 4 February after seeing *Little Malcolm And His Struggle Against The Eunuchs.* "It's marvellous", George said of the play.

"George's lissom blue-eyed

Main pictures: George and Pattie on 12 February at their honeymoon hideaway, a mile from the beach in Barbados. They'd married at Esher Register Office on 21 January, having met on the first day of filming *A Hard Day's Night* in February 1964. Back then the *Daily Sketch* referred to Pattie as a "lissom blue-eyed blonde" and a "vastly successful model". "George is my favourite", Pattie had said of The Beatles. "He's got time to talk to you." John made her laugh by nicknaming her "Battie", the report added, but it was George who won her heart.

Top left and right: Walking to their flight on 8 February, and back at London Airport on the twenty-fifth, George's twenty-third birthday.

blonde."

DAILY SKETCH

No Longer Top of the Pops?

WHEN THE BEATLES finally resurfaced with "Paperback Writer", it was to the tune of a press backlash. Critics delighted in the fact that the single didn't enter each and every one of the nation's charts at No. 1 in its first week of release.

It just "wasn't the right sort of tune for The Beatles"; it was their first record that "you can't dance to"; and, of course, it lacked romance. As Paul explained: "The idea was thought up because my Aunty Mil said we should not do songs about love all the time – even Beethoven got ideas from other people!" But what of the innovative backwards guitar sound on "Rain"? "Easy, of course", declared the *Daily Mirror*'s Patrick Doncaster. "The tape runs the other way for a few bars."

At least the group promoted the single with their only live appearance on *Top Of The Pops* on 16 June, which had come about, said Brian Epstein, "in response to the tremendous demand received from TV companies and fan clubs". And no doubt from the newspapers as well.

After The Beatles had visited Germany and Japan in June and July, followed by the Philippines, and then a tour of America in August, the British press waited eagerly for news of the group's promised end-of-year trek around the UK. Yet none was forthcoming. Back in the summer, the *Daily Sketch* had already posed the question, "Are The Beatles on their way out now?", and as the year wore on the "dilemma" seemed only to get worse, and rumours began to surface that perhaps the group might be splitting up.

"The Beatles have changed their thoughts as their career has been altered by their attitudes in the past", explained manager Brian Epstein, none too clearly. "Naturally this pattern will continue. I'd be a fool to forecast exactly how it will be." Concert promoter Arthur Howes added, "I have no idea when the group will make another tour here. I am not in a position to make them tour. The fans will find new idols. I'm organising The Beach Boys' tour at the moment and that's fairly wild".

But the fans didn't give up that easily. In November, approximately 200 of them laid siege to Brian Epstein's home in Belgravia, handing in a 1,000-signature petition protesting at the lack of British Beatles concerts.

The group's fan club later issued a statement, promising not a tour but a third film. This will begin shooting "at the end of January", added Epstein. The film-versus-touring option was given further credence by Allen Klein, a thirty-four-year-old "Hollywood tycoon" who, on a visit to London, let his intentions be known. "Mr Klein wants The Beatles", said a spokesman. "He thinks they can be film stars. They are stronger together than as individuals. Mr Klein thinks they could be the natural replacement to the Marx Brothers." ■

Left, inset and facing page: The Beatles on the set of the BBC's *Top Of The Pops* on 16 June, their first and final appearance on the show. Even though it was publicised in advance, the *Mirror* counted just six teenagers waiting outside for them to arrive. "The fans just did not turn up as they did a year ago", it was observed.

At the crossroads?

DESPITE ALLEN Klein's thoughts, knockabout comedies no longer appeared to be on the agenda. "The Beatles have now reached the point when they want more time for their own creative work", said their music publisher Dick James.

The end-of-year headlines didn't bode well: "At The Crossroads", "The Sad Dilemma Of Four Very Talented Lads" (both *Daily Mirror*), "Beatles May Not Appear As Group Again" (*Daily Telegraph*), "Beatles Bent On Solo Careers" (*Evening Standard*).

Splitting up? "Nonsense", said Brian Epstein. "I'm sure none of us have deluded ourselves that The Beatles will remain teenage idols for ever", added Northern Songs shareholder Trevor Dawson. "But there's nothing to stop them from remaining popular with all age groups."

Going solo or not, each member had certainly struck out on his own: John had taken a part in Richard Lester's *How I Won The War*, and

> ## "Everything we've done so far has been rubbish, as I see it today."

appeared as a commissionaire on BBC2's *Not Only . . . But Also* with Peter Cook and Dudley Moore (about which performance the *Daily Mirror* commented, "I can think of a hundred actors who could have played it better"); Paul scored the soundtrack for the film *The Family Way*; George spent six weeks studying the sitar in India; while Ringo was said to have "no future plans" other than to keep an eye on his construction business, Brickey Building.

But there was little doubt that change was in the air. "For some time reports have circulated that they want to outgrow their present image", reported the *Daily Express* in November. Which George bluntly confirmed when interviewed in the *Daily Mirror* on the eleventh: "Everything we've done so far has been rubbish, as I see it today. It doesn't mean a thing to what we want to do now."

But talk of the future couldn't allay the reality of the present: when rivals The Beach Boys were voted No. 1 vocal group in the annual *NME* end-of-year readers' poll, Don Short felt he could do little else but conclude in the *Daily Mirror*, "The decline and fall of The Beatles became official last night". ∎

"No interviews", said George as The Beatles flew out to America on 11 August and into the controversy over John's remark that "We're more popular than Jesus now". "I'm worried about what has been going on", John admitted. "But I am not worried about doing this tour." The tour, The Beatles' last, got off to a slow start when their plane was delayed at London Airport for forty-five minutes. To kill time, officials offered a guided tour around the airport's new control room, and showed how the group's army of fans could be monitored from the on-site police station. Paul put on a good show but, try as he might, Ringo couldn't conceal his lack of interest.

Now sporting his new granny-style glasses, on 27 November John joined Peter Cook outside a public convenience in London's Soho to record a comedy sketch for BBC2's *Not Only . . . But Also* (broadcast 26 December). John played the part of Dan, the commissionaire of a gentlemen's night-club, the "Ad-Lav", while Peter Cook took the role of a US TV commentator named Hiram J. Pipesucker Jr. John dressed for the occasion, noted the *Mirror*, in "a long coat, brass buttons, wing collar and top hat", and would only allow Pipesucker into the club upon receipt of a £5 note.

" I can think of a hundred actors who could have played it better."

DAILY MIRROR

CHAPTER FIVE

1967

WITH A CREATIVE REVOLUTION exploding in their heads, The Beatles burned joss-sticks in the studio and meddled with LSD, marijuana, meditation and mysticism. Nothing escaped the imaginative respray: their clothes, the buildings they owned, their cars, their music. Struggling to keep up, the *Sun* called "Strawberry Fields Forever" "the record they can't perform". It was a "musically fascinating" single, but one which "sub-teens may find eccentric and contrived". And last year's predicted downfall now seemed imminent as it failed to reach No. 1. *Sgt. Pepper* offered redemption and "egghead approval" in the summer, but *Magical Mystery Tour* courted more criticism in the winter. But The Beatles'

> ## "What is happening to The Beatles?"
>
> **THOMAS THOMPSON, *NEWS OF THE WORLD***

fashion sense still kept the papers amused; the words on one of John's badges – "Exciting New Offer" – said it all. "Their mode of dress has always been good for a few hundred words' comment", said the *Daily Mirror*. "There were the dark, well-cut suits in which they came to fame. Then their casual wear. The military period. And, lately, the flower look." The flowers were love and peace tokens from God himself; no longer more popular than Jesus, The Beatles were now on equal terms. After meditating with the Maharishi, John announced that, "The kingdom of heaven is like electricity – you don't see it. It is *within* you". To which George added: "I believe in reincarnation. You keep coming back until you get it straight. The ultimate thing is to manifest divinity and become one with the Creator."

And yet John still failed to grasp the material world. After spending thousands redecorating his cars to suit the new mood, he took Beatles' publicist Tony Barrow out for a bumpy ride in his psychedelic Mini. "Why are you bashing the gears and not using the clutch?" enquired Tony. "Are you supposed to, then?" replied John, oblivious to the pedal's function. "I thought that it was just for when you were learning." ■

Fairground Fun-Wagons

IN APRIL, JOHN PAID £1,000 [£10,000 today] for the most talked-about paint job in history, when his two-year-old, £6,000 [£61,000] Rolls-Royce Phantom V, previously establishment black, was transformed into a yellow, swirly fun-wagon of fairground excess.

Above and inset: John's "burly" six-foot-four chauffeur Les Anthony on 25 May displaying John's "anti-taste" Rolls-Royce, newly decorated with dahlias and delphiniums in a £1,000 [£10,000] respray depicting the flowers of autumn. The car is parked in front of Kenwood, John and Cynthia's house in St. George's Hill, Weybridge, Surrey.

The new design was John's own. The theme was October, the month of his birth: the yellow background was decorated with autumnal dahlias, chrysanthemums and delphiniums on the doors, and the zodiacal sign for Libra on the roof. The wheel hubs were red, white, blue and orange, which whirled like kaleidoscope eyes whenever the car was in motion. It was a terrific, tantalising trip – everyone stared as the car drove by, but, with its blackened windows, nobody could see who was inside.

The six-week respray was carried out by James Fallon of J.P. Fallon Ltd, a coachworks company from Chertsey, Surrey, and sixty-two-year-old freelance designer Stephen Weaver (who also charged John more than £3,500 [£35,000] to renovate and decorate an 1874 gypsy caravan John had bought for £100 [£10,000] for his four-year-old son Julian). "It was Mr Lennon's brilliant idea", said Fallon as John's chauffeur Leslie

Anthony picked up the car. "He's ever such a nice young man." Les Anthony might have thought otherwise as onlookers giggled, whistled and even booed as he drove away. Rolls-Royce were unamused. "I cannot recall a Rolls-Royce being decorated in quite this style before", sniffed a spokesman.

The car went on show at Oxfam's Concours d'Elégance rally in Battersea Park on 25 June, and although it attracted the most attention, it won no prizes. "We all agreed it was in extraordinary bad taste and awarded it no points", said judge Commander "Tommy" Thompson. "It seems almost criminal to spoil a beautiful motor in this way." The papers were similarly unamused. "It was neither good taste nor bad taste, just anti-taste", wrote the *Sun*. "It looks like a public raspberry being blown loudly and continously by the young and famous owner of a lot of money . . . Isn't it fun to be modern?"

1967

■ In the City, Northern Songs performed better than expected once again. By October 1967 profits stood at £842,000 [£8,500,000].

■ The Beatles set a new world record in April when they received a US gold disc for 1,000,000 sales of "Strawberry Fields Forever"/"Penny Lane". It was their twenty-second such award.

■ For performing "All You Need Is Love" on the BBC's *Our World* global-TV satellite link-up, The Beatles earned £1,000 [£10,000] per minute for a five-minute song.

■ It was reported in August that the tally of cover versions of Beatles' songs had now passed 10,000.

■ In September, Northern Songs chairman Dick James said that in the last five years The Beatles have earned between £25m and £30m [£303,000,000 today]. But this was an "uneducated guess", he said. "It could be up to £50m [£505,000,000]."

■ In November, *The Great Records* selected *Revolver* as a "dominating disc belonging to the ages".

■ The fact that 13,000,000 viewers watched *Magical Mystery Tour* in December in black-and-white contributed to its "failure". It was repeated in colour in January 1968, but to little effect: there were only 20,000 colour TV sets in the UK at the time.

■ In December, it was reported that the American *Magical Mystery Tour* LP had sold more than 1,600,000 in just ten days.

Left and above: On 24 July, the day before John took delivery of his Roller, a matching gypsy caravan arrived at Kenwood as a birthday present for the Lennons' four-year-old son Julian. Taking the reins en route from the Surrey coachworks to Weybridge were "horse owner Horace Lee, paint firm chief J.P. Fallon and a friend". Not everyone was impressed, and at least one of John's neighbours complained to the residents' association that the caravan was "a hideous monstrosity".

Below and right: At the Motor Show in Earl's Court on 17 October, John became the first customer for the brand new Italian Iso Rivolta S4, the fastest saloon in the world. He and Cynthia spent fifteen minutes looking at the bottle-green car before John told sales manager Maurice Knight, "I'll take it". The price was £6,150 [£62,000].

"It was, as one would expect, an unconventional homecoming."

DAILY MIRROR

Above and left: John, Paul and Georgie Fame in fancy dress at the Cromwellian club in London on 8 January, at the twenty-first birthday for Fame's fiancée Carmen Jiminez.

Facing page, main and centre: "Exciting new offer", said John's badge as he and Paul arrived back at Heathrow Airport on 31 July after a holiday in Greece.

Facing page, top and bottom: Paul and Mal Evans at Heathrow on 12 April after attending Jane Asher's twenty-first birthday party in Denver, Colorado; and Paul meeting Jane at the airport on 29 May, after her spell in the States with the Bristol Old Vic Company.

Above, from top: Ringo on 7 January at his home in Weybridge after being served a writ by his landscape gardener; beautician Vera Bland updates Ringo's hairstyle at Madame Tussaud's on 24 April; and artist Gerald Scarfe on 19 September with his "beautiful models of The Beatles in papier mâché".

A Kind of Poetry

"BEATLES FANS who pooh-poohed The Monkees for not playing their own instruments will be blushing on Friday", wrote Mike Nevard in the *Sun*. He was referring to the release on 1 June of *Sgt. Pepper's Lonely Hearts Club Band*, The Beatles' eighth LP.

Nevard marvelled at the scope of the album: a harp and string quartet on "She's Leaving Home"; Indian dilrubas, tambouras, swordmandels and just one Beatle on "Within You, Without You"; and an entire forty-one-piece orchestra on "A Day In The Life". "It's not for the teenies", he concluded, sealing The Beatles' ascent into the realms of "progressive" music-making.

Jazz singer and critic George Melly dissected the *Sgt. Pepper* recipe for the *Observer*, reckoning the collage effect of the sounds, the sleeve and the concept worked well, but added that "the record is not perfect, even on pop's terms. On the musical side, there is a tendency to overdo the curry powder . . . while on the literary front, the straight psychedelic excursions seem to confuse poetry with woolly nursery surrealism".

The *Sunday Mirror* confirmed that The Beatles were now "the intellectual's favourite pop group", and, like Melly, that "When I'm 64" sounded like a spoof George Formby song. They also recognised poetry but saw no confusion: "The Beatles are here pushing at the boundaries of pop, ranging in space and time, bringing in folk, art, Oriental and music-hall influences . . . it is a planned, balanced programme rather than the usual ad hoc collection. It has humour, pathos, a kind of poetry . . . it will do something to improve the quality of life."

Though thankful for such reviews, EMI appeared bemused by the whole *Sgt. Pepper* concept. Speaking of the LP on behalf of the company, chairman Sir Joseph Lockwood said, "I am sure everyone will want one as a unique souvenir".

At the press launch for the album, held at Brian Epstein's Belgravia home on 19 May, The Beatles once again fascinated followers of fashion with their individual dress sense. John turned up in the most "way-out" gear: "a green lacy shirt and a sporran over his corduroy trousers", reported the *Daily Mirror*. There was a method to his madness, though. "I've got no pockets in my trousers", he explained, "and the sporran is handy to keep your fags in."

At least one paper, the *News of the World*, was completely taken aback. "What is happening to The Beatles?" asked Thomas Thompson on 18 June. "The last time I saw them was at a 1966 concert in New York, standing and moving like forlorn puppets on their platform . . . Now they are grown men and distinctly individual personalities. For a moment I pondered their droopy French moustaches, their bookwormish faces and their bizarre clothes, and considered the extent to which they have gone their separate ways."

The article concluded with Paul saying: "We've reached the point now where there are no musical barriers. Musically, now, this moment, tonight, this is where we are." ■

Left and facing page: The Beatles at the London home of Brian Epstein for the press reception on 19 May to launch *Sgt. Pepper*. They were, observed Judith Simons in the *Daily Express*, "a group now withdrawn from the screaming hysteria of pop world audiences and dedicated to originality and perfection". Beatlemania was finally dead, it was concluded. "I don't think this record will win back the hysterical fringe of youngsters", said the *News of the World*, "but it has some glorious new numbers that reach new frontiers in pop music."

Inset: Paul is approached by photographer Linda Eastman, whom he first met at a Georgie Fame show at the Bag O'Nails club four days before.

"Everything is love."

IN JUNE, PAUL made the "amazing confession" that he'd taken the "heaven and hell" drug LSD. "This opened my eyes to the fact that there is a God", he said in a *Sunday People* interview. "I had never realised what people were talking about when they said God is within you . . . I am not devoting myself to the church, or anything like that."

"To me it is much more personal than that. God is a force we are all part of. But it means that I now believe the answer to everything is love."

The admission brought condemnation from the papers. He was "playing idiot tricks with himself", said the *Sun*. He was a "bloody fool", stated the *Mirror*. But Paul remained unrepentant.

On the fifteenth the *Sunday Mirror* revealed that "cool beyond the dream of cucumbers", The Beatles were unconcerned that there were just "eleven composing days" to go before 400,000,000 people in thirty-one countries tuned in to see them perform a new song on the BBC's *Our World* satellite link-up programme, but it hadn't even been written yet.

"It is a fairly simple love song", George Martin finally revealed, after John and Paul had come up with its basic structure. And weren't the crtitics pleased! "I think it's marvellous", enthused Don Short in the *Daily Mirror*, when he first heard "All You Need Is Love". "Like old soldiers returing to the front with flowers in their berets, The Beatles are battling back again after much criticism." ∎

"One pair of purple trousers stood next to a pair of green trousers next to a pair of stripy trousers next to a vivid orange jacket." So said the *Sunday Times* after witnessing The Beatles' photo-call at EMI Studios in Abbey Road, on 24 June, to publicise the *Our World* broadcast.

"We goofed."

AFTER ATTENDING A PUBLIC LECTURE by the Maharisihi Mahesh Yogi at the London Hilton on 24 August, and travelling by train with him to Bangor, North Wales, for a course in transcendental meditation, The Beatles threw the full weight of their support behind the mystic from the Himalayas known to his followers as His Holiness.

When asked why, John told the *Daily Sketch*'s Anne Nightingale: "Because we've never felt like this about anything else." Transcendental meditation was for everyone, he explained: for younger and older generations, for ordinary householders, for believers in any religion. "There is nothing mystical about mysticism", George would add in a TV interview with David Frost. "It's just people's ignorance."

Admitting that the current "flower power craze" might obscure the real message, John continued in the *Sketch*: "There will be core things that will come out of it which will be worthwhile. Just the love and peace thing is worth it, whatever commercial muck goes on. Now I can see God as a power source or as an energy. All the energy is God. Your own energy and their energy, whether doing god-like things or ungodly things. It's all like one big jelly. We're all in the big jelly."

While in Bangor, The Beatles were told that Brian Epstein had been found dead in his bed at his Chapel Street home. He was thirty-two. "Our meditation has given us confidence to withstand such a shock", said John. "You cannot pay tribute in words", added George. "There is no such thing as death, only in the physical sense. Life goes on. The important thing is that he is OK now."

In September, the *Daily Mirror* appeared incredulous that just weeks after their "flower fashion" phase, The Beatles now seemed to be reviving the "square look" for the filming of *Magical Mystery Tour*, "a colour television effort for worldwide distribution". John and George appeared in a shirt and tie, Paul in a knitted Fair Isle pullover, while Ringo was the most conventional in a pinstripe jacket. But it was all a joke, the paper decided: the point was that the coach trip of the film was an "ordinary" event, and that the four Beatles had vied with each other in "an amusing exercise of sartorial satire". Or had they?

If only the critics had adopted such a wide view when the film was screened on BBC2 on Boxing Day. "No magic in this sad Beatles tour", said Mary Malone in the *Mirror*. "It had no story, no aim. If they were not The Beatles, they could not get a toothpaste merchant to go for this. It was chaotic." The *Express* was even more incensed: "I cannot ever remember seeing such blatant rubbish", wrote James Thomas. "After this corny, confused charade, survival would be difficult for anybody but The Beatles." And in the *Daily Sketch* Robert Ottaway's verdict was, "This witless home movie scotches the myth of their genius for good and all".

"We goofed", admitted Paul. "But you can't win them all. But the Queen's speech wasn't a gas either. Personally, I like the film. It wasn't supposed to be about anything. It wasn't supposed to have a theme or a plot. We did it as a series of disconnected, unconnected events . . . It was our interpretation of 'magical' – and to us, that meant we could do anything." ∎

Top left and facing page, main picture: John, Paul, George, their partners and Mike McGear attend a lecture on transcendental meditation by the Maharishi at the Hilton Hotel on 24 August. The recording session the group had booked for the following evening was hastily cancelled to make way for the weekend seminar.

Left and inset: The Beatles and the Maharishi travel from Euston Station to Bangor for the seminar.

Right: The Beatles leaving the New London Synagogue in Abbey Road, London, on 17 October, after a memorial service for Brian Epstein.

"The Queen's speech

wasn't a gas either."

PAUL McCARTNEY

The new "square-look" Beatles in mid-September, relaxing at the three-star Atlantic Hotel in Newquay, after another day filming *Magical Mystery Tour* (Ringo is pictured here with Aunt Jessie on the coach, facing page, bottom left). Having conceived the project and taken charge of much of its production, Paul (main picture) was already exhausted before being floored in the hotel lounge by the film's youngest participant, a four-year-old tearaway called Nicola Hale, billed simply as The Little Girl.

CHAPTER SIX

1968

"THE BEATLES WERE FORCE-GROWN, like mushrooms in a glass-house. We created the product along with everyone else. We compromised. For years we weren't ourselves. But we are now. We have good intent. We believe we are good people. We believe that our work should show that goodness, and all the rest of it. Amen." This statement from John, quoted in the *Sunday Times*, came in the summer, after months of unsympathetic public scrutiny. There had been the fall-out over *Magical Mystery Tour*; the "mistake" of the Maharishi; the ignoble closure of the Apple Boutique; the end of Paul's five-year relationship with Jane Asher; the collapse of John's own marriage to Cynthia and his public declaration of his love for Yoko Ono. "The violence of the reaction is upsetting", he added, referring to his new romance. "I suppose that I've spoiled my image. People want me to stay in their bag." Remaining firmly in his was Paul: "If the other three were to go freaky looking and wear ridiculous things", he said, "I'd be the one to stay unfreaky just to reassure everyone." Even more "freaky" than yesterday's "flower fashions" was *Yellow Submarine*, "the first example of non-commercial commercial entertainment", as its art director described it. The film delighted some, but was also criticised for its two-dimensional storyline and a multicoloured make-over from the previous summer – it was, after all, inspired by a song from 1966 and Pepperland characters dreamed up in 1967. *Sgt. Pepper's Lonely Hearts Club Band* was described in *Time* magazine as "their classic moment, fusing the pop spirit and an astoundingly eclectic range of sounds into a harrowing but harmonious whole". But try telling John Lennon that. "As far as I'm concerned", said John, "*Sgt. Pepper* was just a phase. It's last year's music. This year's will be simpler."

"Are The Beatles hell-bent on destroying themselves?"

ANNE NIGHTINGALE, *DAILY SKETCH*

A Walking Charity?

"WE'VE GOT ALL THE MONEY WE NEED", Paul told the *Evening Standard* on 24 February. "I've got the house and the cars and all the things that money can buy. So now we want to start directing this money into a business . . . When Brian died we had to take a look at what we consisted of, and who owned bits of us, and then we got the idea of not only doing it for ourselves but for everyone."

That was the philosophy behind their new company Apple, but a twenty-year-old Leicester University student called John Eades soon tested the measure of Paul's philanthropy. After bombarding him with telegrams and camping outside his St. John's Wood home, Eades persuaded Paul to support a Leicester University students' campaign protesting about inadequate funding for their campus arts festival.

Appearing at the students' London press conference obviously peeved, Paul stressed he would not be donating money to the cause, and neither would he be visiting Leicester. "The conning stops here", he said. "I don't know anything about the festival in detail, and really this is a complete publicity gimmick." Did he often get calls asking for his help? a reporter asked. "Quite often", Paul replied, mentioning two writers who'd recently asked for money to spend time drafting their "great work". "I told them to get a job, and then start writing", said

Paul. "That way, they'd feel much better afterwards. After all, I'm not a walking charity."

It had been a different story a few months before, when both Paul and John backed another artistic adventurer, the painter Jonathan Hague. Unlike Eades, Hague didn't have to pester The Beatles – he'd been to art college with John – and easily secured a generous sponsorship worth £1,500 [£14,500]. "We always like to help old friends", said John.

Jonathan and John were evidently on the same wavelength: the two had been reunited at the Maharishi's retreat in Bangor and Hague's subjects ranged from van Gogh to Mick Jagger to The Beatles themselves.

"They told me that they'll give me what publicity they can get with their own names", Hague told the *Daily Mail*, adding the deal would last two years. "Identification with any other pop group might have devalued my work", he concluded. "But not The Beatles – they have sufficient connotations of culture."

Left, top: Paul and Jane Asher at the London Pavilion on 4 January for the premiere of *Here We Go Round The Mulberry Bush*, the book of which was written by Beatles biographer Hunter Davies. The Pavilion had hosted the premieres of both *A Hard Day's Night* and *Help!*

Left, bottom: Paul and Jane at the airport, back from India via Tehran, on 26 March.

Inset: George returning from Bombay with Magic Alex on 16 January, after recording the *Wonderwall* soundtrack.

1968

■ In July the *Daily Sketch* reported that John was "fed-up" with his psychedelic Rolls-Royce and had sold it in America for $50,000 [£21,000 then, £202,000 today]. He threw in four unreleased Beatles' tapes as part of the deal.

■ Sales of Beatles' singles around the world now stood at over 210,000,000, the *Evening News* reported in July.

■ Issued in August, "Hey Jude" had sold 3,000,000 copies in America by the end of October, becoming The Beatles' sixteenth US million-seller.

■ In the first week of release, British and American sales of "Hey Jude" earned Northern Songs £12,365 [£120,000] in royalties, reported the *Sunday Mirror*.

■ The changing faces of The Beatles meant that their Madame Tussaud's wax figures were updated once again in November. The five changes since 1964 had cost Madame Tussaud's £800 [£8,350].

■ First-week sales of *The Beatles* (the "White Album") were "phenomenal", Dick James told the *Evening Standard* in December: 333,000 in the UK and over 1,000,000 in the US.

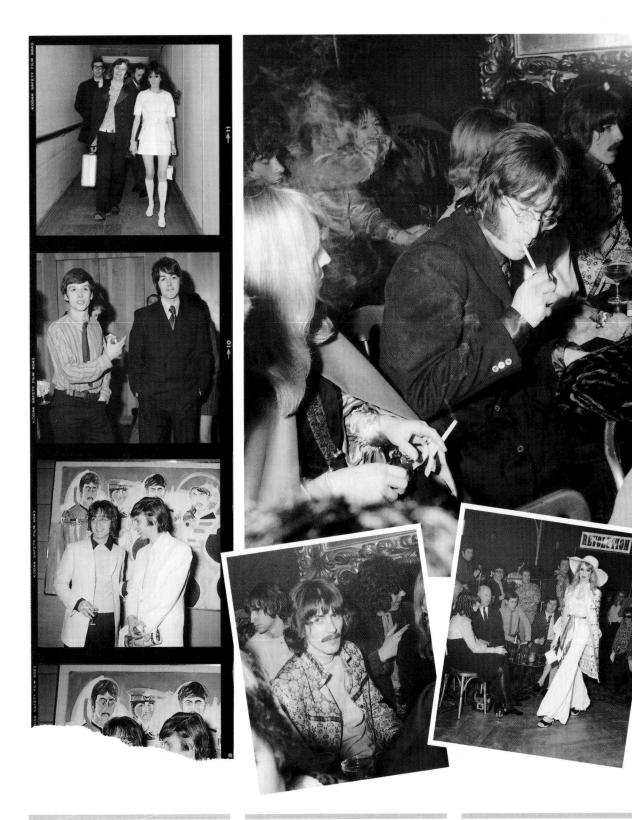

Hand-to-hand combat

ON 15 FEBRUARY, John and Cynthia, and George and Pattie, flew out to New Delhi, India, for a three-month course in transcendental meditation with the Maharishi Mahesh Yogi. Paul and Ringo and their respective partners followed a few days later.

Naturally, the press went too, and such was their thirst for news about the goings-on behind the gates of the Maharishi's Himalayan retreat that it led to "almost hand-to-hand combat between journalists and the Guards of the High Priest", as the *Sunday Mirror* reported. Peace was only restored when Apple's Mal Evans appeared at the gates with a report on The Beatles' daily routine.

They rose at 6.00 a.m., he dictated, to take the traditional Hindu cold-water bath. They then meditated for an hour-and-a-half, before appearing individually in front of the Maharishi to

> ## "It is good. You feel super."

explain their experiences. The guru then interpreted their feelings and helped guide them towards the inner peace which was the goal of transcendental meditation. A forthcoming level in the five-step plan would be to meditate non-stop for thirty hours without food, drink or sleep. Ringo stayed in India for ten days before flying home, but Paul proved more resilient, lasting five weeks. Returning to London, he concluded that the trip had been a success. "In meditation", he revealed, "you turn inwards. It is good. You feel super."

After nearly two months, John suddenly gave up the final fortnight of his study and flew back to Heathrow Airport on 12 April, leaving George the only Beatle on the course. Speaking a few days later John said: "It did us a great deal of good. We learned a lot from it."

However, in May, while he and Paul were in New York to announce the launch of their company, Apple, Paul declared that while The Beatles still believed in meditation, they had lost faith in the Maharishi. "We made a mistake", he said. "We thought there was more to him than there was. He's human. We thought at first he wasn't." ∎

Above, from top to bottom: Ringo and Maureen leave Heathrow on 15 May for the Cannes Film Festival; Leicester arts protagonist John Eades tries hard, but fails to appease a peeved Paul at the Royal Garden Hotel, Kensington, on 5 February; John, his old Liverpool College of Art mucker Jonathan Hague and

Hague's portrait of The Beatles, at the Royal Institute Gallery on 7 December 1967. After sponsoring Hague to the tune of £1,500 [£14,500], John bought his Beatles painting for £450 [£4,350], only to change his mind and swap it, in a moment of spontaneity, for a picture of the King of Baghdad.

Above, main picture and insets: John, with his John Sebastian sideburns, lights a fag at a Quorum fashion show at the Revolution club in Mayfair on 18 January. He and George were there to see Pattie model designs by Ossie Clarke and Alice Pollock.

Stepping stones of life

"A YEAR AGO", declared the *Daily Mail* in May, "George announced that meditation would solve the problems of life." But now, he also denounced the Maharishi. A *Daily Mail* reporter visited George at his home in Esher, Surrey, and found him wearing "an Indian-style orange-flowered trouser suit" and ready to speak his mind.

"The whole situation is delicate", George said. "I have not broken with the thoughts of meditation. I have only broken with the Maharishi and his ideas of making the whole thing subject to mass-media. We believe that he took advantage of the publicity that we gave him by going to him in the Himalayas. Life is a process of finding stepping stones and treading on them. The Maharishi was one of the stepping stones in our life."

"The disenchantment of The Beatles with the Maharishi has burst yet another of their bubbles", Bunny Lewis wrote in *Reveille* the following month. "It is a fact of life that only the affluent can afford to indulge in such highfalutin' ideas. The rest of us are obliged to get plastered at the

> ## "The Maharishi's main trouble was a tendency to spread something subtle in a gross way."

pub and face up to the problems slightly worse for wear the next day."

Paul's comment that The Beatles had thought the Maharishi "more than human" was "naive but understandable", added Lewis, who went on to quote George as saying: "You can't produce mass cosmic consciousness. The Maharishi's main trouble was a tendency to spread something subtle in a gross way."

Ringo — "certainly the least talented of The Beatles, but surely the most down-to-earth" — won a proverbial slap on the back for claiming the Maharishi's course was "just like Butlin's on the Ganges", while Cilla Black, whom Lewis revealed was "never a devotee", was even more prosaic. According to *Reveille*, "she always thought that meditation was 'going to the loo with a big pile of papers, sitting there and reading them all'".

Above: Ringo and Cilla Black at the BBC TV Theatre in Shepherd's Bush on 5 February polishing up their soft-shoe shuffle for the first episode of *Cilla*, broadcast the following day. The show also received support from Paul, who wrote the "Step Inside Love" theme tune.

Far left: Ringo at EMI Studios on 7 March, voicing his appreciation for sound engineer Geoff Emerick, recipient of a Grammy Award for Best Technically Engineered Album (*Sgt. Pepper*).

Left: Ringo toasting the town with Mike Todd Jnr and Elizabeth Taylor at a private screening of *Around The World In 80 Days*, at the Coliseum Cinerama in London on 23 March. The screening was hosted by Elizabeth Taylor and Richard Burton.

Top: Half of The Beatles, their wives and Pattie's sister Jenny Boyd at Heathrow Airport on 15 February, bound for the Maharishi's Himalayan retreat in India.

Above: Ringo and Maureen and their pet poodle Tiger, given to them as a wedding present back in 1965, at Heathrow on 2 January, en route to quarantine-free Liverpool.

Left: The other half of The Beatles, plus Jane and Maureen, leave London for India on the nineteenth.

"We may even rival Woolworth's in the end."

JOHN LENNON

Left: George and Pattie, Ringo and Maureen and Jane's brother, Peter Asher, at Heathrow on 18 June, returning from San Francisco where George had been taking part in the Ravi Shankar film *Raga*.

Above: John, dressed in white and clutching a Panama hat, and Paul in green and blue, prepare to fly to New York on 11 May to announce the launch of Apple. Between them is head of Apple Electronics, Magic Alex.

"A very beautiful girl."

THERE WAS A McCARTNEY MARRIAGE on 7 June, but it wasn't the long-rumoured union of Paul and Jane Asher. Rather, it was Paul's younger brother Michael – Mike McGear of The Scaffold – who tied the knot with hairstylist Angela Fishwick at the parish church of Carrog, a village in Merioneth, North Wales. Paul was best man.

Paul and Jane's intentions had been the topic of public discussion since December 1963, when they were first photographed as a couple. In March 1964 they refuted claims that they were engaged, but in June 1965 Paul announced "I will be the third Beatle to marry", only to deny it a day later. On 15 August the same year, Jane told the papers, "Yes, I am marrying Paul", and at a New York press conference in August 1966, Paul had said he and Jane were "probably" going to get married. It was reported that Jane was to fly out to Seattle, where The Beatles were on tour, for a ceremony at the British Consulate. A wedding cake had even been delivered to the group's hotel, the Olympic. Back in London, Paul once again scotched the stories.

The couple finally announced their engagement in December 1967, when Paul bought Jane an emerald and diamond ring. Seven months later, on 21 July 1968, it was all over. "I haven't broken it off, but it's finished", Jane said on the BBC TV chat show *Dee Time*. "I don't want to say anything about it."

Reporters flocked to Paul's father's house at Gayton on the Wirral, doorstepping Paul for a statement. Would he be seeing her again? "I'm just going to wait and see what happens", he replied, before adding: "Jane is still a very beautiful girl." ∎

Above: Best man Paul kisses the bride after the marriage of Mike McCartney and Angela Fishwick at the parish church in Carrog, North Wales, on 7 June.

Centre and facing page: Best man Paul with Jane Asher pose alongside the bride and groom.

Right: Roger McGough (with glasses) and John Gorman of The Scaffold join the McCartney brothers at the wedding reception.

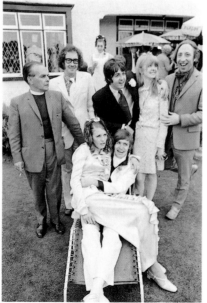

Our own brass band

ON 12 JUNE, the *Daily Mirror*'s Don Short filed a piece about Apple Corps Ltd, The Beatles' new company which comprised four divisions of electronics, merchandise, films and music – a company which is "brushing aside the conventions of big business", he said.

"We're going to have our own brass band", Paul announced, and within weeks he could be found practising the idea on the streets of Saltaire, north of Bradford, Yorkshire – recording the award-winning Black Dyke Mills Band for an Apple single.

Old associates were given new jobs in the new company. "In a year's time", said Paul, "the organisation will be so big that the friends we have will be immersed by friends we never dreamed of."

The project was an expensive one – it had been created with "half a million pounds left in the kitty after Beatlemania ended", noted Short

> ## "They thought . . . they were just dealing with four clowns."

– and it boasted forty-nine members of staff on the payroll. But, admitted John, the business needed structuring. "We've been looking for a (Lord) Beeching figure to come in and organise us", he said. "We had several of 'em in, but they just didn't come up to scratch. The chaps we had in the interview were bigoted. They thought they knew everything and that they were just dealing with four clowns. But we saw through them right away and felt we couldn't offer any one of them the £20,000 [£193,000] per year we were prepared to pay."

The Beatles treated the venture seriously – both John and Paul arrived for work at Apple's fifth-floor offices on Wigmore Street, central London, soon after nine o'clock in the morning – and money appeared to be no object. An Apple executive told Short that he would be disappointed if the company didn't turn over "£10 million sterling within the next three years" – although this was far from guaranteed. "We could fall flat on our faces", conceded John. "So what if we do? But at the moment we can only see success." ■

This page: John and his new girlfriend Yoko Ono at the opening of his *You Are Here* exhibition in London's West End on 1 July.

Facing page: Paul (and Martha the Old English sheepdog) conducts Britain's most famous brass band, the Black Dyke Mills, at Victoria Hall, Saltaire, on 30 June.

Inset, below right: John and Yoko are remanded on bail on 19 October at Marleybone Magistrates Courts for possession of cannabis.

"I am in love with her."

JOHN OPENED *You Are Here* on 1 July at the Robert Fraser Gallery in London's West End. Described by the *Daily Mirror* as a "highly off-beat" art exhibition, the show consisted of twenty-four charity collection boxes ranging from the National Canine Defence League to the Sons of the Divine Providence. There was also an upturned hat "for the artist", and a huge circular white canvas ("a portrait of nothing"), in the centre of which could be found the exhibition's title. "I want it to replace 'Kilroy was here' on toilet walls", John said of the phrase. "It makes more sense."

John dedicated the event to the "bottoms girl" Yoko Ono, the Japanese artist and film-maker famous for her *Film No. 4*, which consisted of 365 close-ups of bare backsides. John and Yoko, both dressed in white, launched the show by cutting loose the same number of white, helium-filled balloons. "I pronounce these balloons high", said John.

"I pronounce these balloons high."

"I got the idea for this exhibition from a childhood memory", John told the newspapers. "I remembered how excited I was when I found a balloon in a field when I was little." A ticket carrying the invitation "Write to John Lennon" was attached to each and every balloon.

Reporters were more interested in Yoko Ono, and what she meant to John Lennon. When asked he replied simply, "I am in love with her". Did this mean that his marriage to Cynthia was over? "Not legally", he said. "I'm not talking about my marriage. I don't want to say anything about it. It complicates matters."

Speculation about Cynthia's involvement with another man was later dismissed as "rubbish". "At the moment she is living like a nun", said a friend. "She hardly ever goes out or sees anyone. She is very upset about everything."

Pop-op Art Nouveau

THE UNRULINESS OF BEATLEMANIA was briefly revisited in London on 17 July, and Piccadilly Circus was brought to a standstill, as 10,000 fans waited for the group to arrive at the premiere of *Yellow Submarine*. The animated film was, according to its art director Heinz Edelmann, "a psychedelic cornucopia of styles ranging from pop-op to art nouveau".

Acutely wary of Beatles' films after *Magical Mystery Tour*, the critics were divided. "Mythological figures in their own life-size", chortled the *Daily Express*, "the four hoarse men of the twentieth century apocalypse are portrayed here in cartoon form, and the medium does justice to the legend." The *Daily Mirror* claimed the film was: "Highly enjoyable while the creators' collective imaginations hold out. But when they flag, which is about three-quarters of the way through, the sub sinks . . . But the techniques are impressive, the use of colour wild and there is always the pounding attraction of The Beatles' beat and the genuine sweetness of their music."

"The film is a panorama of everything that every colour supplement has done in the last two years", sniffed *The Times*, "and as such is already a trifle dated before it hits the screen. For this reason, it seems unlikely to please the really sophisticated, but should do well with those panting along slightly in the rear of fashion." Commercially, though, it didn't do well. "Shocked" by adverse box-office returns, the Rank Organisation began a war of words with distributors United Artists over the film's viability and, in early August, dropped it from fifteen of its London cinemas.

"I thought we were lumbered with real bad business when I first saw it", said Harvey Marriner, assistant manager of the Holloway Odeon. "I mean, it's rubbish, isn't it?

"The 85 minute film was the first picture presentation by Apple", the *Daily Mirror* was quick to point out, "the new Beatles' empire which closed down its first fashion boutique last week because of lack of trade." More ominous, however, was the *Daily Mail*'s comment: "Now a question mark hangs over the future of the group and friends believe the four will eventually go their separate ways, pursuing individual interests." ∎

Facing page: Paul, George and Ringo at the Bowater House Cinema in Knightsbridge on 8 July, as The Beatles, minus John, attend a press preview of the animated movie, *Yellow Submarine*.

Left: John and Yoko, Ringo and Maureen and George and Pattie arrive at the London Pavilion in Piccadilly on 17 July for the premiere of the film.

Inset, above: Beatlemania, 1968 style. And the hysteria wasn't just confined to the streets of London. While many critics were harsh about *Yellow Submarine*, for the Reverend Jim Smith of the Holy Trinity Church, Middletown, Lancashire, it was a religious experience. "I can see in the film", he said, urging his parishioners to see it, "Beatle equivalents of the fall of the Garden of Eden, the fall of man and the coming of the Saviour."

"Jagger is the Charlie Chaplin of rock'n'roll."

JOHN LENNON

On 10 and 11 December, John and Yoko took part in the filming of The Rolling Stones' *Rock And Roll Circus*, a £50,000 [£480,000] colour TV "costume spectacular" filmed at Intertel Studios in Wembley, which also featured The Who. Backed by the Dirty Mac, a pick-up band comprising Keith Richard, Eric Clapton and Jimi Hendrix's drummer Mitch Mitchell, John sang one song, "Yer Blues", from *The Beatles*, before jamming with Yoko on a free-form piece they referred to later as "Her Blues". The Stones intended the film to be screened at Christmas, but perhaps wary of the reaction to *Magical Mystery Tour*, their interest in it waned shortly after completion and the broadcast was cancelled.

Above: At rehearsals on the tenth; left to right, Bill Wyman, Charlie Watts, Keith Moon, Brian Jones, Yoko, Julian Lennon, John and Eric Clapton.

Facing page: John the clown, Yoko the witch, The Rolling Stones in costume and members of Robert Fossett's Circus on 11 December.

CHAPTER SEVEN

1969

"THERE WAS A BIT OF BOTHER among the group in the studio", a spokesman told the papers when a dispute between John and George during the shooting of *Let It Be* was rumoured to have come to blows. George later denied any violence. "Beatles only throw bowls of soup over each other when they get mad", he told Don Short in the *Daily Mirror*. Playing together on the roof of Apple for the *Let It Be* cameras in January was The Beatles' only public appearance of the year, and even then only those working in the area around Savile Row witnessed the event.

The group began the decade looking similar, doing the same things, wanting the same things, but had ended up as four completely different individuals married, as Ray Connolly pointed out in the *Evening Standard*, to four completely different women moving in wildly different social circles: Ringo to his "fan girlfriend from Liverpool", George to his "beautiful London model", Paul to his "homely New York photographer", and John to his "avant-avant garde Japanese artist". The highlight of Paul's public year was his and Linda's wedding in March. Ringo's was his co-starring role with Peter Sellers in *The Magic Christian*, while George went on tour as a sideman to American blue-eyed soul duo Delaney & Bonnie, was busted for drugs with Pattie, and brought the spiritual sounds of the Radha Krishna Temple into the charts with "Hare Krishna Mantra".

John and Yoko were denounced as the "outstanding nutcases of the world" after dressing all in white, and then all in black; for spending a week in bed in front of the cameras for their honeymoon; for inventing "Bagism"; for making genre-defying films and music; and for making high-profile protests against violence, war, capital punishment and their records slipping down the charts. Summing up in the summer, John said, "I am not a traditionalist, as everybody knows". ■

> **"The Beatles are now little more than a fond memory."**
>
> RAY CONNOLLY, *EVENING STANDARD*

"He loves me."

THE NEWS THAT PAUL WAS TO MARRY Linda Eastman was first announced by *Disc & Music Echo,* only to be picked up by the newspapers on 6 February. The ceremony was to take place in the next ten days, the reports said. Linda was described as "a New York society girl", and the "27-year-old green-eyed, honey-blonde daughter of the Picasso-collecting American Lee Eastman". She was a divorcée, it was added, with a daughter called Heather, aged six.

Just days before, actress Olivia Hussey, the seventeen-year-old star of *Romeo And Juliet*, had suggested to the *Sunday Mirror* that she might be the one to snap up the last bachelor Beatle. "After he took me out, Paul said he loves me", she revealed. "What more can I say?"

News of the actual wedding date only leaked out when Linda booked Marylebone Register Office on 11 March for the following morning. "Yes, it's true. I am getting married", said Paul outside the Apple offices at 3 Savile Row. "But I'm saying nothing more at the moment." The other three Beatles weren't informed and didn't attend. Paul's best man was his brother Mike McGear, while Apple's Peter

Brown and Mal Evans acted as witnesses. "All I wanted was a quiet ceremony between Linda and myself", Paul said afterwards. "It doesn't concern anybody else." The 800 largely female fans who gathered outside Marylebone Register Office on the big day thought otherwise, and there were tears and hysterics reminiscent of 1964. Although the decision to wed and the act itself had appeared sudden (the ceremony lasted just four minutes), Paul was adamant he wasn't rushing into anything. "I believe in marriage seriously enough to have got married", he said after receiving a blessing from the Reverend Noel Perry-Gore at the parish church in St. John's Wood. ■

Top: Paul and Linda leave Savile Row in Paul's Mini on 6 April, after a recording session at the Apple Studios.

Far left: The day before the marriage, Paul confirms his intentions to Don Short of the *Daily Mirror*.

Left: Leaving Apple's offices with Peter Asher, Jane's brother, after announcing plans to marry Linda.

Inset: Paul and Linda at the film premiere of *Isadora* on 4 March at the Odeon, St. Martin's Lane, London.

1969

■ In January, the *Daily Mirror* revealed that Northern Songs had spent over £800,000 [£7,300,000] on the Lawrence Wright music publishing catalogue of 4,000 oldies, among them George Formby's "When I'm Cleaning Windows".

■ In March, an American promoter offered The Beatles £1,500,000 [£13,755,000] for four concerts. They refused. "When the government takes 19s 6d out of every £1 we earn, how can we feel inspired?" asked Paul. "It's enough to make us wanna go broke."

■ After John told *Disc & Music Echo* that "all of us will be broke in the next six months", George said in the *Sun*: "Nineteen and six out of every pound goes to Harold. I could earn a million and be lucky to keep, say, a thousand."

■ After a five-month battle, Associated Television gained control over Northern Songs in September by buying a 15 per cent share block owned by a City investment group. The £10,000,000 [£91,700,000]

deal left ATV with 53 per cent, and John and Paul with 47 per cent between them.

■ When *The Beatles Illustrated Lyrics* was published in October, Italian censors objected to the proliferation of naked women and asked for 130 of the 160 pictures to be removed.

■ In December another offer to tour the States in 1970 was rejected. The twelve-show deal was worth up to £2,500,000 [£23,000,000], but "The Beatles are not interested in touring again", said Apple.

Top left: The new Mr and Mrs McCartney and Linda's daughter Heather with the Reverend Noel Perry-Gore, outside St. John's Wood Church on 12 March after the blessing.

Above and far left: Paul, Linda and Heather at the wedding reception at the Savoy Hotel, London. There was no suggestion of "the weird and wonderful garb that is synonomous with Beatle living", declared the *Evening News*. "He was in a dark suit and silk tie, she in a yellow belted coat a good two inches below her knees."

Left: The newly-weds at home in Cavendish Avenue, St. John's Wood, on 17 March.

"They look like a couple

# of chumps, or chimps."

DONALD ZEC

Eight days after Paul wed Linda, John and Yoko were married in Gibraltar in a ceremony which lasted just three minutes. "It was all very quick, quiet and British", said John. "We thought it was impossible for a Beatle to marry secretly. We have proved it's not."

It was the "love story of the decade", announced the *Evening Standard*, and to share in that love, John and Yoko invited the world's press and "interested parties" along to their seven-day bed-in, beginning on 25 March

in Room 902 of the Hilton Hotel, Amsterdam. "We're staying in bed as a protest against all the war and violence in the world", explained John. "It's a happening, a bed production. We want people to stay in bed or grow their hair instead of getting involved in violence. Hair is nice. Hair is peaceful."

The *Mirror*'s Donald Zec reluctantly took up the offer and sat on the bed with his "hairy hosts". "Taken at face value", he told them, "you're either a couple of

nuts who ought to be put away, or you're on to a pretty smart angle with a good profit at the end of it." And what would the other Beatles think? "Ringo would think it pretty funny", John replied. "George would understand. But Paul would be cynical like you."

Below: John and Yoko, unhappy at being turfed out of bed by Portuguese chambermaid Maria de Soledade Alves.

The God-figure

RINGO SPENT MUCH OF THE YEAR filming Terry Southern's satire *The Magic Christian* with Peter Sellers. Shooting began in March and the movie was premiered in December.

The month before Ringo told the *Daily Mirror Magazine*: "I made the film because I wanted to make it. I didn't have to make it, not to earn my living, or to change anything. It's not me trying to leap out, saying I'm 21 and going to change my name to Richard and all that nonsense."

He was well aware of the limitations of his appeal, he admitted: "No matter what you do on your own, you're always Ringo the Beatle. And that's all right. You can't get away from it ever."

Although rarely outspoken on such issues, Ringo then voiced his opinion on peace and religion, subjects usually associated with John and George. "I find it very hard to change the world", he said. "But we're all together, this generation. We're all in. I think that's why pop's so big at the moment. Everyone took up guitars instead of guns – we're the first ones to have a chance."

He'd tried Christianity, he added, but remained unconvinced. "I believe in reincarnation", he said. "You come down to do something. I just follow the path. After this life I'll go somewhere else and I'll get taught something else. There are a lot of stages, and in the end you become one with the god-figure."

George took his own religious questing one stage further when he signed the London chapter of the Radha Krishna Temple to Apple for the traditional devotional chant "Hare Krishna Mantra". He was unconcerned whether or not the record was a hit (although it was, selling some 70,000 copies per day in September, landing the Temple an appearance on *Top Of The Pops*). More important was the message behind it.

"We, The Beatles, have a definite job in society", George told the *Sun* in April. "We are trying to communicate – that's the only thing. We want to make people more aware of what's going on in the world. You see, we represent something that the establishment don't want – change. We're trying to speed up that change and that's what they fear."

He went on to say: "I stopped going to church when I was thirteen, maybe twelve. I had to go through all that Indian scene to find that God is all the good things in life. But then the people teaching religion don't know God themselves, and when religion is forced on you by people who don't know the Truth, it just turns them away." ∎

Left, top: George with members of the twelve-strong Radha Krishna Temple at a press reception at Sydenham Hill, southeast London on 28 August, to announce the Apple release of "Hare Krishna Mantra".

Left, centre: John, George and Ringo with Yoko, Pattie and Maureen watching Bob Dylan on stage at the Isle of Wight Pop Festival on 1 September. The Beatles and The Rolling Stones were due to stay with Dylan at the sixteenth-century farmhouse he'd rented on the island. "The Beatles have asked me to work with them", Dylan said on 27 August.

Left, bottom: George and Eric Clapton backstage with Delaney & Bonnie at the Town Hall, Birmingham on 3 December. The two guitarists took low-key roles on the couple's "And Friends Tour" of the UK. George later flew to Denmark with the tour, for three dates in Copenhagen.

Inset: George and Patti leave Esher & Walton Magistrates' Court on 31 March after facing charges for the possession of drugs.

Top: Ringo and Peter Sellers throw money around at the roulette table at Les Ambassadeurs in London on 4 May at a *Magic Christian* party.

Above: Ringo and Peter Sellers wave to photographers as they set sail while filming on board the *QE2* on 16 May.

Right: Ringo as Youngman Grand and Peter Sellers as Sir Guy shooting the free-money-in-the-septic-pool scene for the end of the film on the Thames Embankment, near Belvedere Road, on 16 June.

Unselling

"BAGISM" — conducting oneself beneath the shroud of a large white bag — was a way of preventing people's preoccupation with physical appearances: "It helps get rid of racial prejudice", as John explained to the *Daily Mirror*. "Bag" was also the name of a new company he and Yoko set up to disassociate themselves from the activities of the other three Beatles.

It was "John Lennon of Bag" who returned his MBE to the Queen on 25 November in protest at Britain's support of the Nigeria–Biafran and Vietnam wars – and against his "Cold Turkey" single "slipping down the charts". In returning the medal John announced his withdrawal from "the Establishment game".

"I personally sold out", he told the press from his Bag office at Apple, "because the whole MBE was an embarrassment to me. It was a humiliation. I don't believe in royalty and titles. But I went through with it to make it. I have made it now and I'm unselling, if you like."

"The 'Cold Turkey' quip", he added, "was a gimmick or a twist to take the seriousness out of it. All anti-war movements make the same mistake. They get too serious and get battered to pieces."

Ringo was the only Beatle to publicly support John's action. "We were awarded the MBE for peaceful efforts", he told the *Daily Express*, "and John's is being returned in an effort for peace. We don't see ourselves as grumpy old colonels in Berkshire acting in anger."

On 15 December John fronted the hastily assembled twelve-man Plastic Ono Band Supergroup at a "Peace for Christmas" charity concert in aid of UNICEF, at the Lyceum Ballroom in the Strand, London. Joining him onstage was Yoko (in a bag), Eric Clapton, Billy Preston, and the husband-and-wife team of Delaney & Bonnie.

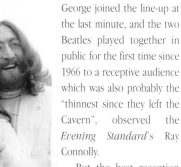

George joined the line-up at the last minute, and the two Beatles played together in public for the first time since 1966 to a receptive audience which was also probably the "thinnest since they left the Cavern", observed the *Evening Standard*'s Ray Connolly.

But the best reception John and Yoko received all year was a small, third-column piece in the *Daily Mirror*, which praised the "surprise treat" they gave seventy-three partially sighted children of Holmrook Special School in Liverpool back in June. The newly-weds had been staying with John's son, Julian, and Yoko's daughter, Kyoko, at the home of John's aunt, Harriet Birch, in nearby Gateacre, when they stopped by the school en route to Scotland to sign autographs and encourage "smiles and cheers". Even Donald Zec couldn't criticise. ■

Left, top: Travelling as Mr and Mrs Chambers, and dressed in their *Apotheosis* capes and hats, John and Yoko leave Heathrow on 16 December for Toronto, to hold talks about their "great festival for peace", planned for July 1970.

Left: John and Yoko with Mr and Mrs Hanratty and Edith Whicher, a member of the campaign to clear Hanratty's name, at Apple on 10 December. John called a press conference in his Bag office to announce that he and Yoko would be making a film about the Hanratty case.

Inset: With Yoko's daughter, Kyoko, at Heathrow on 24 May en route to the Bahamas.

Facing page, top: John and Yoko bringing smiles to Holmrook Special School in Liverpool on 26 June. Note the children's giveaway *Daily Mirror* paper caps.

Facing page, centre: George, Bagism and John and Yoko at the Lyceum on 15 December.

Facing page, bottom: John and Yoko at Apple with his Bag letter to the Queen returning his MBE on 25 November; and Bagism in action at Speaker's Corner on 14 December.

Man of the decade

ON 14 DECEMBER, the usually vocal John and Yoko made "A Silent Protest For James Hanratty", the man hanged in 1962 for the murder of Michael Gregsten on the A6. Two anonymous stand-ins, wrapped from head to foot in a large white linen bag and wearing a sign declaring, "Britain Murdered Hanratty", stood for five minutes at Speaker's Corner in Hyde Park, as James Hanratty Snr proclaimed his son's innocence and called for a public enquiry into the case. This couple later drove Mrs and Mrs Hanratty to 10 Downing Street, where a petition was handed in citing four additional witnesses not present at Hanratty's trial. Earlier John had announced he would soon be making an anti-capital punishment film for TV.

Later in the month the Lennons launched another film, *Apotheosis*, in which, reported the *Sunday Telegraph*, "they seek to portray themselves almost entirely spiritually". The half-hour widescreen movie, shown at the ICA, featured the couple for only five minutes at the beginning as they prepared to go up in a hot-air balloon. The remaining footage starred the sky and clouds above southern England as the balloon drifted over Basingstoke, Hampshire. "It's

> ## "The *Mirror* chooses . . .
> ## The Clown Of The Year."

the best thing we've done to date", Yoko said, although they later reshot the film. "John and I are thinking more and more in spiritual terms."

Spirituality was the last thing on Donald Zec's mind. At the end of the year ITV included John in an hour-long documentary *Man Of The Decade*, which also featured John F. Kennedy and Ho Chi Minh; the ever-cynical columnist weighed in with a half-page editorial, "Today the *Mirror* chooses . . . The Clown Of The Year".

"John Lennon means well", he began. "But it is not what goes on in the mind, rather what comes out of the mouth, that sets Mr. Lennon slightly apart from his fellow human beings. Such influence as Lennon might have had upon his generation – music apart – has probably been lost in the corners of that daft white bag . . . Mr Lennon's cry is 'Peace!' How about giving us some, chum?"

The caption to the solemn picture of John accompanying the article ran to just one word: "Lennon."

"It means 'release from earthly life'."

SUNDAY TELEGRAPH

John and Yoko, dressed from head to toe in black capes, hoods, balaclavas and gloves, filming *Apotheosis 2* in the snow in the Market Square, Lavenham, Suffolk, on 5 December. This was the couple's second attempt to make their 35mm hot-air-balloon film, having rejected a previous attempt shot over Basingstoke, Hampshire. According to the *Sunday Telegraph*, the word Apotheosis means "release from earthly life, or more strictly deification or canonisation".

DAILY Mirror

Lennon-McCartney song team splits up

5d. Friday, April 10, 1970   No. 20,616

PAUL IS QUITTING THE BEATLES

Swing to Labour .. but Tories are still in command

LABOUR scored morale-boosting gains in the Greater London Council elections early today—but the swing was not nearly enough to wrest control from the Tories.

They captured three seats from the Tories at Camden—and one at Greenwich.

First results showed an average swing to Labour of just over 3 per cent. compared with 1967, when the seats were last contested.

By VICTOR KNIGHT

At 2 a.m. it was still doubtful whether Labour would be able to gain the eleven seats needed to win control of the Inner London Education Authority.

But there was no doubt that they would not be able to gain the 32 seats necessary to control the Greater London Council itself.

Hampered

Labour held their seats at Barking, Tower Hamlets, Hackney and Newham. The Tories held Harrow, Havering, Hillingdon, Kingston, Sutton, Waltham Forest, Merton, Bexley, Redbridge and Richmond. Labour's recovery was hampered by the low turnout in many areas.

Bad weather played a significant part in discouraging people from voting.

With half the results declared, the average turnout was 35 per cent.

Outside London, the Tories were consolidating their hold on the counties.

With results from twenty-eight counties in, the Tories were showing 40 gains in seats and Labour 28.

The Tories gained control of one county, East Suffolk, where previously Independents held sway.

One of Labour's biggest disappointments was in Northumberland, where they had high hopes of regaining control.

They lost three seats to the Tories—though they picked up one from an Independent.

Union Movement candidates came bottom of the poll in several London boroughs.

Labour did well in Buckinghamshire, gaining six seats from the Tories.

The "Homes Before Roads" candidates made very little impression.

In Lancashire there was a swing of 6 per cent to Labour in Premier Harold Wilson's constituency of Huyton.

Counts

The voting in London was for 97 seats on the Greater London Council. Three more—in Hammersmith—are to be contested on April 27.

A record total of 491 candidates contested the 100 seats.

Only 26 of the London constituencies did their counts last night.

Five—Ealing, Westminster, Barnet, Croydon and Kensington and Chelsea—declare today.

Mrs. Lena Townsend,

Date

Labour also did well in London by successfully fighting off a Tory challenge at marginal Islington.

It is unlikely that this week's council results will help Premier Harold Wilson to decide the date of the General Election.

Labour leaders can point to some modest gains.

But the low polls in many areas make it extremely difficult to reach hard-and-fast conclusions.

It is still possible that Mr. Wilson will call a General Election in May or June—particularly if there is a good reaction to next week's Budget.

But most MPs are forecasting that the Prime Minister will wait at least until October.

leader of the Inner London Education Authority, lost her seat at Camden.

A significant feature of the London poll was the large number of Independents standing under varying descriptions.

All of them were annihilated.

The Liberals, though not doing as badly as the Independents, also made a poor showing.

McCartney . . . a policy deadlock.

By DON SHORT

PAUL McCARTNEY has quit the Beatles. The shock news must mean the end of Britain's most famous pop group, which has been idolised by millions the world over for nearly ten years.

Today 27-year-old McCartney will announce his decision, and the reasons for it, in a no-holds-barred statement.

It follows months of strife over policy in Apple, the Beatles' controlling organisation, and an ever-growing rift between McCartney and his song-writing partner, John Lennon.

In his statement, which consists of a series of answers to questions, McCartney says:

"I have no future plans to record or appear with the Beatles again. Or to write any more music with John."

Last night the statement was locked up in a safe at Apple headquarters in London's Savile-row, Mayfair—in the very rooms where the Beatles' break-up began.

The Beatles decided to appoint a "business adviser." Eventually they settled for American Allen Klein.

His appointment was strongly resisted by Paul, who sought the job for his father-in-law, American attorney Lee Eastman.

After a meeting in London Paul was out-voted 3-1 by John, and the other Beatles, George Harrison and Ringo Starr.

Since the Klein appointment, Paul has refused to go to the Apple offices to work daily.

He kept silent and stayed at his St. John's Wood home with his photo-

Clash over the running of Apple

grapher wife Linda, her daughter Heather, and their own baby, Mary.

Close friends tried to pacify John and Paul. But August last year was the last time they were to work together — when they collaborated on the "Abbey Road" album.

Films

There were other elements that hastened Paul's decision to quit. John Lennon, on his marriage to Yoko Ono, set out on projects of his own. Ringo went into films, and George stepped in as a record producer.

Today McCartney will reveal his own plans for a solo programme.

Early today an Apple spokesman denied that Paul McCartney had left the Beatles.

But he said that there were no plans "at the moment" for any more recordings.

The seventies got off to a sour start as the *Mirror* announced the end of The Beatles on 10 April. The music had ceased to be important, and the split was over matters of "policy", wrote Don Short. "I have no further plans to record or appear with The Beatles again", said Paul. "Or to write any more music with John."

Chronology

1963

1 January   The Beatles return from their last residency at the Star-Club, Hamburg

2 January   Opening date on a week-long tour of Scotland

11 January   Single release: "Please Please Me"/"Ask Me Why"

19 January   National TV debut on *Thank Your Lucky Stars*

2 February   Opening night of first UK tour, supporting Helen Shapiro

9 March   Opening of UK tour supporting Chris Montez and Tommy Roe

10 March   The Beatles take over as headline act on Montez/Roe tour

12 March   The Beatles play three nights as a trio due to John's heavy cold

22 March   LP release: *Please Please Me*

11 April   Single release: "From Me To You"/"Thank You Girl"

4 June   Launch of BBC radio series *Pop Go The Beatles*

3 August   Last concert at the Cavern Club, Liverpool

9 August   First issue of *The Beatles Book* monthly magazine

23 August   Single release: "She Loves You"/"I'll Get You"

10 September   Donald Zec begins his "Big Beat" series in the *Daily Mirror* with a feature on The Beatles; they win Top Vocal Group of the Year at the Variety Club Awards at the Savoy Hotel

15 September   The Beatles share the bill with The Rolling Stones at the annual *Great Pop Prom* at the Royal Albert Hall

13 October   Live appearance on *Sunday Night At The London Palladium* on ITV

19 October   "Fantastic scenes" at the Pavilion Garden Ballrooms, Buxton, Derbyshire

1 November   Opening night of *The Beatles Autumn Tour* in Cheltenham, Gloucestershire

2 November   *The Daily Mirror* reviews the Cheltenham show with the headline "Beatlemania!"

4 November   The Beatles top the bill at the Royal Variety Performance

10 November   The Beatles are disguised as policemen to get into the Hippodrome, Birmingham

20 November   Single release: "I Want To Hold Your Hand"/"This Boy"

22 November   LP release: *With The Beatles*

12 December   Paul's gastric flu forces two concerts at the Guildhall, Portsmouth, to be cancelled

21 December   ITV broadcast the second all-Merseyside edition of *Thank Your Lucky Stars* (the first was in June)

24 December   *The Beatles' Christmas Show* begins a sixteen-night season at the Astoria Cinema, Finsbury Park, London

1964

4 January   The critics are divided after a clip of The Beatles is shown on US TV

14 January   The Beatles (minus Ringo) fly to Paris for a residency the Olympia Theatre

7 February   The Beatles are greeted by up to 10,000 screaming fans at John F. Kennedy Airport

9 February   73,000,000 American viewers watch The Beatles play live on the *Ed Sullivan Show*

11 February   Washington Coliseum, their debut concert in the US

13 February   From New York, The Beatles fly to Miami Beach, Florida, for a week

25 February   George receives an estimated 15,000 cards for his twenty-first birthday

2 March   Filming of *A Hard Day's Night* begins. George meets model and film extra Pattie Boyd

19 March   The Beatles collect their 1963 Showbusiness Personalities of the Year award from Harold Wilson at the Variety Club of Great Britain

20 March   Single release: "Can't Buy Me Love"/"You Can't Do That"; The Beatles appear on *Ready, Steady, Go!*

23 March   The Duke of Edinburgh presents The Beatles with Carl-Alan awards

27 March   John, George and their partners are guests of US millionaire Bernard McDonagh at Dromoland Castle, Limerick, Ireland

8 April   George and Pattie and Paul and Jane Asher attend a party for Anthony Newley and Joan Collins in London

23 April   John fails to speak, prompting cries of "Poor show!" and "Shame!", at a Foyle's literary luncheon in his honour at the Dorchester Hotel

23 April   John and Ringo attend Roy Orbison's twenty-eighth birthday party in London

26 April   Headlining at the NME poll-winners concert at Wembley

29 April   The Beatles are photographed with their Madame Tussaud's waxworks in London

6 May   ITV screen their own TV special *Around The Beatles*

3 June   As Ringo is taken ill, Jimmy Nicol temporarily replaces him as The Beatles' drummer

6 July   London premiere of *A Hard Day's Night*

10 July   Northern premiere of *A Hard Day's Night*

10 July   Single release: "A Hard Day's Night"/"Things We Said Today"

10 July   LP release: *A Hard Day's Night*

12 July   The Beatles play the Hippodrome, Brighton, at the first of five summer concerts at British seaside resorts

23 July   The Beatles appear in the charity show *The Night of A Hundred Stars* at the London Palladium

19 August   A month-long tour of the US begins in San Francisco

17 September   Earning around £1,785 per minute, The Beatles are paid $150,000 to play the Kansas City Municipal Stadium on their day off

27 September   Ringo judges eleven unknown bands on BBC2's *It's Beat Time*

9 October   Motown star Mary Wells joins The Beatles for their UK tour, beginning at the Gaumont Cinema, Bradford

8 November   First concert in Liverpool for nearly a year at the Liverpool Empire

27 November   Single release: "I Feel Fine"/"She's A Woman"

30 November   Ringo visits the *Melody Maker* offices in Fleet Street to see "I Feel Fine" debut at No. 1 as the weekly chart is compiled

1 December   Ringo holds a press conference about his tonsils

4 December   LP release: *Beatles For Sale*

24 December   *Another Beatles Christmas Show* begins at the Odeon Cinema, Hammersmith

1965

15 January   Ringo dances "The Skip" with Cilla Black at a *Melody Maker* party in London

11 February   Ringo marries Maureen Cox

12 February   Mr and Mrs Starr hold a press conference at their honeymoon hang-out in Hove, East Sussex

24 February   The Beatles begin filming *Help!* in the Bahamas

9 April   Single release: "Ticket To Ride"/"Yes It Is"

14 April   Filming of the communal house sequence for *Help!* in Twickenham

26 April   Ex-Beatle Pete Best is interviewed in the *Daily Mirror*

27 April   Stand-in Beatle Jimmy Nicol is declared bankrupt in London

3 May   Filming *Help!* on Salisbury Plain

12 June   The Beatles' MBEs are announced

23 July   Single release: "Help!"/"I'm Down"

29 July   *Help!* is premiered in London

1 August   The Beatles play live on ITV's *Blackpool Night Out*

6 August   LP release: *Help!*

13 August   Two-week tour of the US begins when 55,600 see them perform at New York's Shea Stadium

27 August   The Beatles meet Elvis Presley in Beverly Hills

3 December   Single release: "We Can Work It Out"/"Day Tripper"

3 December LP release: *Rubber Soul*
3 December The Beatles' last UK tour begins at the Odeon Cinema, Glasgow
16 December ITV broadcast *The Music Of Lennon & McCartney*

1966

21 January George marries Pattie Boyd in Esher
8 February George and Pattie fly to Barbados for their honeymoon
10 June Single release: "Paperback Writer"/ "Rain"
16 June The Beatles' first and final appearance on *Top Of The Pops* performing "Paperback Writer" and "Rain"
5 August Single release: "Eleanor Rigby"/ "Yellow Submarine"
5 August LP release: *Revolver*
11 August The Beatles fly out to Chicago for their final US tour
9 December LP release: *A Collection Of Beatles Oldies*
26 December The BBC broadcasts Peter Cook and Dudley Moore's *Not Only But Also* in which John takes a brief cameo role as a commissionaire in a comedy sketch

1967

8 January John and Paul attend a fancy dress party hosted by Georgie Fame in London
17 February Single release: "Strawberry Fields Forever"/ "Penny Lane"
8 April John visits J.P. Fallon coachworks in Surrey to discuss the repainting of his Rolls-Royce in the style of gypsy caravan
15 May Paul meets Linda Eastman at a Georgie Fame show at the Bag O'Nails club in London
19 May Brian Epstein hosts a press reception at his Belgravia home to launch *Sgt. Pepper's Lonely Hearts Club Band*

1 June LP release: *Sgt. Pepper's Lonely Hearts Club Band*
19 June Paul admits on TV that he has taken LSD
24 June Photo-call and press conference for the *Our World* TV broadcast
25 June 400,000,000 watch The Beatles perform "All You Need Is Love" on the world's first global satellite TV link-up
7 July Single release: "All You Need Is Love"/ "Baby, You're Rich Man"
31 July John and Cynthia and Paul and Jane return from Greece dressed in the latest "flower fashions"
24 August All four Beatles, plus Pattie and Jane, attend a lecture on transcendental meditation at the Hilton Hotel by the Maharishi Mahesh Yogi; the following day they all travel to Bangor, North Wales, for a weekend seminar
27 August Brian Epstein is found dead at his house at 24 Chapel Street, Belgravia, London

11 September A Beatles coach party, including a camera crew and forty-three passengers, set off for the West Country to film *Magical Mystery Tour*
24 November Single release: "Hello Goodbye"/ "I Am The Walrus"
7 December John and Paul sponsor an exhibition of paintings of ex-Liverpool College of Art student Jonathan Hague

1968

25 January John and George attend an Ossie Clark fashion show in London, at which Pattie is one of the models
5 February Paul is "conned" into attending a press conference for Leicester University students' annual arts festival
6 February Ringo appears live on Cilla Black's *Cilla* TV show

15 February John and Cynthia and George and Pattie fly to India for the Maharishi's course in transcendental meditation
19 February Paul and Jane and Ringo and Maureen fly out to India
15 March Single release: "Lady Madonna"/ "The Inner Light"
11 May John and Paul fly to New York to publicise Apple
7 June Paul and Jane Asher attend Mike McCartney's wedding in North Wales

30 June Paul records the Black Dyke Mills Band for Apple
1 July John's first art exhibition *You Are Here* opens in London
17 July Premiere of *Yellow Submarine* in London
30 August Single release: "Hey Jude"/ "Revolution"
8 November John and Cynthia Lennon divorce
22 November LP release: *The Beatles*
11 December John and Yoko appear in The Rolling Stones *Rock And Roll Circus*

1969

2 January The Beatles begin filming *Get Back*, later released as *Let It Be*
17 January LP release: *Yellow Submarine*
30 January The Beatles play together for the last time in public on the Apple rooftop for *Get Back/ Let It Be*
1 March Ringo begins filming *The Magic Christian* with Peter Sellers
12 March Paul marries Linda Eastman at Marylebone Register Office
20 March John marries Yoko Ono at the British Consulate in Gibraltar
25 March John and Yoko begin their bed-in at the Hilton Hotel, Amsterdam

11 April Single release: "Get Back"/ "Don't Let Me Down"
30 May Single release: "The Ballad Of John And Yoko"/ "Old Brown Shoe"
29 June John, Yoko and their children Julian and Kyoko, begin a motoring holiday of Scotland, stopping off at Holmrook Special School for partially sighted children in Liverpool
26 September LP release: *Abbey Road*
28 August George attends a press conference in Sydenham, southeast London, for the Radha Krishna Temple
1 September John and Yoko, George and Pattie and Ringo and Maureen see Bob Dylan in concert at the Isle of Wight Pop Festival
17 October Single release: "Cold Turkey" by the Plastic Ono Band
31 October Single release: "Something"/ "Come Together"
25 November John returns his MBE to the Queen
2 December George joins the Delaney & Bonnie & Friends tour in Sheffield
5 December John and Yoko re-enact scenes from their film *Apotheosis* for the cameras
14 December John and Yoko appear in a white bag at Speakers' Corner in "A Silent Protest" about the hanging of James Hanratty
15 December The Plastic Ono Supergroup, including John and George, plays a charity concert in London

1970

6 March Single release: "Let It Be"/ "You Know My Name (Look Up The Number)"
10 April Paul McCartney announces that he has left The Beatles. "I have no further plans to record or appear with The Beatles again", he said in a statement
8 May LP release: *Let It Be*

Acknowledgements

This book is dedicated to Cindy England.

For help with this project, thanks to Caroline for
all the encouragement, to Fionna for the
friendship, and to Mark for being there.
To the dynamic trio of Phil Smee, Chris Westhorp
and Will Steeds, without whom this book
would not have been possible.
Thank you to Hugh Gallacher, Alisdair
MacDonald, Victor Crawshaw, Tony Ward and
Nick Kent at Mirror Group.
To Pete Nash, Keith Badman and Jacques
Volcouve for their knowledge and enthusiasm,
and to Mark Lewisohn for his unmatchable
research and invaluable books.
Special thanks to Miles for his Foreword.
Final thanks to my *Record Collector* colleagues
Pat, John and Peter for putting up with me
all these years.

**Above: Big Mal Evans dismantles Ringo's tiny drum kit
after The Beatles' concert at the Washington Coliseum
on 11 February 1964.**

**Overleaf: The Beatles relaxing between takes during
filming of *A Hard Day's Night* at the Scala Theatre, London,
on 31 March 1964.**

Bibliography

Braun, Michael. *Love Me Do! The Beatles Progress*
(Penguin, 1964)
Davies, Hunter. *The Beatles*
(William Heinemann, 1968)
Hine, Al. *The Beatles In Help!*
(Mayflower-Dell, 1965)
Lewisohn, Mark. *The Beatles Live!*
(Pavilion, 1986)
Lewisohn, Mark. *25 Years In The Life*
(Sidgwick & Jackson, 1987)
Lewisohn, Mark. *The Complete Beatles Chronicles*
(Pyramid, 1992)
Lewisohn, Mark, Schreuders, Piet & Smith, Adam.
The Beatles' London
(Hamlyn, 1994)
Rayl, AJS & Gunther, Curt.
A Hard Day's Night In America
(Sidgwick & Jackson, 1989)
Wiener, Allen J.
The Beatles, The Ultimate Recording Guide
(Aurum Press, 1993)

UK Periodicals:
*Daily Express, Daily Herald, Daily Mail,
Daily Mirror, Daily Mirror Magazine,
Daily Sketch, Daily Telegraph, Daily Worker,
Evening News, Evening Standard,
Financial Times, News of the World,*
the *Observer,* the *People, Reveille,* the *Sun,
Sunday Citizen, Sunday Mirror,
Sunday Telegraph, The Times*

International Periodicals:
Le Figaro, Newsweek, New York Times, Time